STARGIRL

Jerry Spinelli

WITH RELATED READINGS

THE EMC MASTERPIECE SERIES

Access Editions

EMC/Paradigm Publishing
St. Paul, Minnesota

Staff Credits:

Laurie Skiba
Managing Editor

Lori Coleman
Editorial Consultant

Brenda Owens
High School Editor

Nichola Torbett
Associate Editor

Rebecca Palmer
Associate Editor

Jennifer Anderson
Assistant Editor

Jennifer Wreisner
Senior Designer

Paul Spencer
Art and Photo Researcher

Valerie Murphy
Editorial Assistant

Marie Couillard
Copy Editor

Parkwood Composition
Compositor

Anne Todd
Educational Writer

Cover: © Ryan McVay/Getty Images

Library of Congress Cataloging-in-Publication Data

Spinelli, Jerry
    Stargirl / Jerry Spinelli.
       p. cm. — (The EMC masterpiece series access editions)
       Summary: In this tale of the perils of popularity, the courage of non-
conformity, and the thrill of first love, an eccentric student named
Stargirl changes Mica High School forever. Includes related readings
      ISBN 0-8219-2504-0
      [1. Individuality—Fiction. 2. Popularity—Fiction. 3. Eccentrics and
eccentricities—Fiction. 4. High schools—Fiction. 5. Schools—Fiction.
6. Arizona—Fiction.] I. Title. II. Series.

PZ7.S75663 St 2002
[Fic]—dc21

                                        2002023003

ISBN 0-8219-2504-0
Copyright © 2003 by EMC Corporation

Published by EMC/Paradigm Publishing
875 Montreal Way
St. Paul, Minnesota 55102
800-328-1452
www.emcp.com
E-mail: educate@emcp.com

Printed in the United States of America.
    5 6 7 8 9 10 xxx 11 10 09 08 07

Table of Contents

Jerry Spinelli

Jerry Spinelli was born on February 1, 1941, in Norristown, Pennsylvania. As a child he read Bugs Bunny comics and a few sports novels. He wishes he'd read more. Spinelli played baseball in junior high and high school. He first decided to become a writer in high school after a poem of his about a football game was published in the local newspaper.

Jerry Spinelli

Spinelli graduated from Gettysburg College in 1963. He received his M.A. from John Hopkins University in 1964. During college Spinelli wrote four books for adults. He could not get any of them published.

After college Spinelli served in the Naval Reserve from 1966 to 1972. He married Eileen, also a writer, in 1977. Still aiming for an adult market, Spinelli sent his fifth book to publishers. They returned it because the main character was a thirteen-year-old boy. Spinelli decided to try a children's publisher. The children's publisher offered him a contract. Spinelli's first book, *Space Station Seventh Grade,* was published in 1982.

Spinelli says that ideas for his books come easily for him, but good ideas are hard. When students ask where he gets his ideas for his books, Spinelli replies, "From you. You're the funny ones."

Books by Jerry Spinelli
The Bathwater Gang
The Bathwater Gang Gets Down to Business
Blue Ribbon Blues: A Tooter Tale
Crash
Do the Funky Pickle
Dump Days
Fourth Grade Rats
Jason and Marceline
Knots in My Yo-Yo String: The Autobiography of a Kid
The Library Card
Maniac Magee
Night of the Whale
Picklemania

Time Line of Jerry Spinelli's Life

On February 1, Jerry Spinelli is born in Norristown, Pennsylvania.	1941
Spinelli graduates from Gettysburg College.	1963
Spinelli receives his M.A. from Johns Hopkins University.	1964
Spinelli serves in the Naval Reserve.	1966–1972
Spinelli marries Eileen, also a writer.	1977
Space Station Seventh Grade is published.	1982
Who Put that Hair in My Toothbrush? is published.	1984
Night of the Whale is published.	1985
Jason and Marceline is published.	1986
Dump Days is published.	1988
The Bathwater Gang and *Maniac Magee* are published.	1990
Fourth Grade Rats, There's a Girl in My Hammerlock, and *School Daze: Report to the Principal's Office* are published. *Maniac Magee* wins a Newbery Medal.	1991
The Bathwater Gang Gets Down to Business and *Do the Funky Pickle* are published.	1992
Picklemania is published.	1993
Tooter Pepperday is published.	1995
Crash is published.	1996
The Library Card and *Wringer* are published.	1997
Blue Ribbon Blues: A Tooter Tale and *Knots in My Yo-Yo String: The Autobiography of a Kid* are published. *Wringer* wins a Newbery Honor Award.	1998
Stargirl is published.	2000

Characters in
Stargirl

Main Characters

Stargirl Caraway. Stargirl's birth name is Susan Julia Caraway. Stargirl is a quirky tenth grader who attends Mica Area High School after having been home-schooled by her parents. She dresses and acts differently from the other students at MAHS.

Leo Borlock. Leo is the narrator of *Stargirl*. He is the director/producer of *Hot Seat,* a cable television show produced at the high school. He falls in love with Stargirl Caraway.

Kevin Quinlan. Kevin Quinlan is Leo's best friend and the host of *Hot Seat.*

Archie (Archibald) Hapwood Brubaker. Archie was a paleontologist and university teacher. Now he is retired and teaches the Mica kids on an informal basis at his home. Leo goes to Archie to seek advice.

Minor Characters

Hillari Kimble. She is a student at MAHS. She is Wayne's girlfriend. She does not like Stargirl. She is one of the jury members on *Hot Seat* when Stargirl is the victim.

Wayne Parr. He is a student at MAHS. He is Hillari's boyfriend. He is the most popular boy in school—someone whom others follow in deciding what to wear and how to act. He wants to become a model.

Dori Dilson. Dori is Stargirl's first true friend. Dori, a ninth grader at MAHS, writes poems in her notebook and didn't have any friends until Stargirl.

Mr. and Mrs. Caraway. They are Stargirl's parents. Mr. Caraway works at Mica Tronics and Mrs. Caraway makes costumes for movies.

Alan Ferko. Ferko is the first MAHS student that Stargirl sings "Happy Birthday" to in the lunchroom.

Anna Grisdale. Anna is a student at MAHS. Stargirl attends Anna's grandfather's funeral.

Raymond Studemacher. Raymond is the first student to stop shunning Stargirl. He dances with her at the Ocotillo Ball.

Mallory Stillwell. Mallory is captain of the cheerleaders at MAHS.

Brent Ardsley. Brent is the leading scorer on the MAHS basketball team.

Jennifer St. John. She is a juror on *Hot Seat*.

Damon Ricci. He is a juror on *Hot Seat*.

Mike Ebersole. He is a juror on *Hot Seat*.

Becca Rinaldi. She is a juror on *Hot Seat*.

Renee Bozeman. She is a juror on *Hot Seat*.

Ron Kovac. Ron is a superstar on the Sun Valley basketball team.

Danny Pike. Danny, a nine-year-old boy, almost died after a bike accident. Stargirl sends him a new bike.

Peter Sinkowitz. Peter is a young boy who lives across the street from Stargirl. She is writing his biography.

Mr. Robineau. Mr. Robineau is *Hot Seat's* faculty advisor.

Mr. McShane. He drives Stargirl and Leo to the oratorical state finals. He is MAHS's faculty representative.

Chico. Chico is the handheld close-up camera used on *Hot Seat*.

Cinnamon. Cinnamon is Stargirl's pet rat.

Barney. Barney is a 60-million-year-old Paleocene rodent skull.

Señor Saguaro. It is a cactus at Archie's house. Archie often speaks to Señor Saguaro.

Guy Greco. He is the bandleader at the Ocotillo Ball.

Uncle Pete. Pete is Leo's uncle who got him interested in porcupine neckties.

Echoes:

Themes from Stargirl

First keep the peace within yourself, then you can also bring peace to others.

—Thomas à Kempis

You give but little when you give of your possessions. It is when you give of yourself that you truly give.

—Kahlil Gibran

I expect to pass through this world but once; any good thing therefore that I can do, or any kindness that I can show to any fellow creature, let me do it now; let me not defer or neglect it, for I shall not pass this way again.

—Stephen Grellet (attributed)

Do all the good you can,
By all the means you can,
In all the ways you can,
In all the places you can,
At all the times you can,
To all the people you can,
As long as ever you can.

—John Wesley

and if ever I touched a life I hope that life knows
that I know that touching was and still is and always will be the true revolution

—Nikki Giovanni

Whoever is happy will make others happy too. He who has courage and faith will never perish in misery!

—Anne Frank

Conduct your blooming in the noise and whip of the whirlwind.
                                        —Gwendolyn Brooks

We never know how high we are
Till we are called to rise
And then, if we are true to plan
Our statures touch the skies.

                                        —Emily Dickinson

Speak in French when you can't think of the English for a thing—turn out your toes when you walk—and remember who you are!

                                        —Lewis Carroll

There are two ways of spreading light: to be
The candle or the mirror that reflects it

                                        —Edith Wharton

Freedom and constraint are two aspects of the same necessity, which is to be what one is and no other.

                                        —Antoine de Saint-Exupéry

Preface

For Leo Borlock in the novel *Stargirl*, high school is a stressful place. He and everyone else around him face pressure about fitting in—a situation that is reflected in thousands of middle schools and high schools across the country.

Each day, teenagers everywhere are faced with hundreds of choices—from what extra-curricular activities to participate in to what clothes to wear and which people to hang out with. Teenagers get guidance from parents, teachers, peers, and their own inner voices. During the high school years, teenagers struggle to be accepted at school and in their peer groups as they also strive to become independent.

But some young adults question the cost of conforming to be well liked. One boy who became popular after changing his appearance wrote about his experience in an essay entitled "Is Image Everything?":

> The image and confidence worked, and I began to accumulate friends. I thoroughly enjoyed my new-found popularity, and for a while, actually believed I was happy. But as I examined my situation more closely, I questioned my new friendships. Some people with whom I had dreamed of being friends with just a year before hadn't given me the time of day then. I was pretty much the same person, personality-wise, maybe more mature, but basically the same. Why hadn't they noticed me then? Were my friendships just because of my new image?
>
> —James B., Teen Ink/The Young Authors Foundation, Inc., 2002

Most kids are fully aware of how peer pressure causes people to act differently than they otherwise might. James went on to say, "I learned how to be just as false with them as they were with me." He ended the essay by stating, "It disgusts me sometimes, but I have been sucked in and don't want to stand out as different." Even though he was aware that he was not being himself, James chose to continue bowing to peer pressure. That is not uncommon. It also is not limited to teens. Many adults follow the same sorts of behaviors. Peer pressure, conformity, and popularity influence the decisions and behaviors of many adults.

People who do choose not to conform to the ways of others—people who rebel, in a sense—are different from other people in many ways. They may choose to dress, speak, and act differently. They may also find that they are different from other nonconformists. Some people like the attention they get from being different, even if the attention is negative. Others feel shy or uncomfortable and tend to be loners. Still others make conscious decisions to be themselves and not allow peer pressure to affect them.

Social status—being popular or being an outsider—can affect a person's happiness. But that does not mean that all popular people are happy. Fitting in does not automatically cause a person to be content. Similarly, being an outsider does not guarantee that a person is unhappy. Being conscious of your decision to be conventional or to go your own way and then being satisfied with that decision are both important in making you a happy person.

As young adults mature, they begin to see beyond peer pressure and find that their own values are more important. They also see that it is wrong to hurt or put down people who do not conform. Outright mocking and laughing, shunning, and throwing insults are just some of the ways that people can and do hurt other people who are considered outsiders.

In addition to the immediate effects that these behaviors have on victims, some far-reaching consequences also can occur. People outside the so-called popular groups may already have feelings of low self-esteem. If they are continually taunted or humiliated, their low self-esteem may lead to depression or even suicide. Of course, low self-esteem, depression, and suicide do not only affect outsiders. These issues also affect many other teens who are trying to discover who they are and where they fit in—even teens who are considered popular.

Growing up is a huge challenge. Even still, most young people get through the experience just fine and are happy and healthy. Common sense is a good rule to follow. Think about how you would feel if you were in someone else's place. How would you want others to treat you? What could you do to make it better for the person on the outside?

In Jerry Spinelli's novel *Stargirl,* Stargirl Caraway is the kind of girl who refuses to conform. As Leo gets to know her, he realizes he has to decide how to be around her. Stargirl, and Leo's reaction to her, will change his life in some very big ways.

Porcupine Necktie

When I was little, my uncle Pete had a necktie with a porcupine painted on it. I thought that necktie was just about the neatest thing in the world. Uncle Pete would stand patiently before me while I ran my fingers over the silky surface, half expecting to be stuck by one of the quills. Once, he let me wear it. I kept looking for one of my own, but I could never find one.

I was twelve when we moved from Pennsylvania to Arizona. When Uncle Pete came to say good-bye, he was wearing the tie. I thought he did so to give me one last look at it, and I was grateful. But then, with a dramatic <u>flourish</u>, he whipped off the tie and draped it around my neck. "It's yours," he said. "Going-away present."

◀ What going-away present does Uncle Pete give to Leo?

I loved that porcupine tie so much that I decided to start a collection. Two years after we settled in Arizona, the number of ties in my collection was still one. Where do you find a porcupine necktie in Mica, Arizona—or anywhere else, for that matter?

On my fourteenth birthday, I read about myself in the local newspaper. The family section ran a regular feature about kids on their birthdays, and my mother had called in some info. The last sentence read: "As a hobby, Leo Borlock collects porcupine neckties."

Several days later, coming home from school, I found a plastic bag on our front step. Inside was a gift-wrapped package tied with yellow ribbon. The tag said "Happy Birthday!" I opened the package. It was a porcupine necktie. Two porcupines were tossing darts with their quills, while a third was picking its teeth.

I inspected the box, the tag, the paper. Nowhere could I find the giver's name. I asked my parents. I asked my friends. I called my uncle Pete. Everyone denied knowing anything about it.

◀ What happens when Leo asks his family and friends if they gave him the package?

At the time I simply considered the episode a mystery. It did not occur to me that I was being watched. We were all being watched.

---

words for everyday use
flour • ish (flər' ish) v., wave in the air. *She took off her new scarf with a <u>flourish</u>, hoping I'd notice it.*

Chapter 1

"Did you see her?"

That was the first thing Kevin said to me on the first day of school, eleventh grade. We were waiting for the bell to ring.

"See who?" I said.

"Hah!" He craned his neck, scanning the mob. He had witnessed something remarkable; it showed on his face. He grinned, still scanning. "You'll know."

There were hundreds of us, milling about, calling names, pointing to summer-tanned faces we hadn't seen since June. Our interest in each other was never <u>keener</u> than during the fifteen minutes before the first bell of the first day.

I punched his arm. "Who?"

The bell rang. We poured inside.

I heard it again in homeroom, a whispered voice behind me as we said the Pledge of Allegiance:

"You see her?"

I heard it in the hallways. I heard it in English and Geometry:

"Did you see her?"

Who could it be? A new student? A spectacular blonde from California? Or from back East, where many of us came from? Or one of those summer makeovers, someone who leaves in June looking like a little girl and returns in September as a full-bodied woman, a ten-week miracle?

And then in Earth Sciences I heard a name: "Stargirl."

I turned to the senior slouching behind me. "Stargirl?" I said. "What kind of name is that?"

"That's it. Stargirl Caraway. She said it in home-room."

"*Stargirl?*"

"Yeah."

▶ What was Stargirl wearing when Leo saw her at lunch?

And then I saw her. At lunch. She wore an off-white dress so long it covered her shoes. It had ruffles around the neck and cuffs and looked like it could have been her great-grandmother's wedding gown. Her hair was the color of sand. It fell to her shoulders. Something was strapped across her back, but it wasn't a book bag. At first I thought it was a miniature guitar. I found out later it was a ukulele.[1]

She did not carry a lunch tray. She did carry a large canvas bag with a life-size sunflower painted on it. The lunchroom was dead silent as she walked by. She stopped at an empty table, laid down her bag, slung the instrument strap over her chair, and sat down. She pulled a sandwich from the bag and started to eat.

Half the lunchroom kept staring, half started buzzing.

Kevin was grinning. "Wha'd I tell you?"

I nodded.

"She's in tenth grade," he said. "I hear she's been home-schooled till now."

"Maybe that explains it," I said.

Her back was to us, so I couldn't see her face. No one sat with her, but at the tables next to hers kids were cramming two to a seat. She didn't seem to notice. She seemed <u>marooned</u> in a sea of staring, buzzing faces.

Kevin was grinning again. "You thinking what I'm thinking?" he said.

I grinned back. I nodded. *"Hot Seat."*

Hot Seat was our in-school TV show. We had started it the year before. I was producer/director, Kevin was on-camera host. Each month he interviewed a student. So far, most of them had been honor student types, athletes, model citizens. Noteworthy in the usual ways, but not especially interesting.

Suddenly Kevin's eyes <u>boggled</u>. The girl was picking up her ukulele. And now she was strumming it.

◀ *What is* Hot Seat?

---

1. **ukulele.** Small guitar of Portuguese origin

words for everyday use	ma • roon (mə' rün) v., place or leave in isolation or without hope of ready escape. *When I started a new school half-way through the year, I felt <u>marooned</u> amid all the new faces.*	bog • gle (bä' gəl) v., start with fright or amazement. *My eyes <u>boggled</u> when I saw an unexpected A+ on my term paper.*

And now she was singing! Strumming away, bobbing her head and shoulders, singing, "I'm looking over a four-leaf clover that I overlooked before." Stone silence all around. Then came the sound of a single person clapping. I looked. It was the lunch-line cashier.

And now the girl was standing, slinging her bag over one shoulder and marching among the tables, strumming and singing and strutting and twirling. Heads swung, eyes followed her, mouths hung open. Disbelief. When she came by our table, I got my first good look at her face. She wasn't gorgeous, wasn't ugly. A sprinkle of freckles crossed the bridge of her nose. Mostly, she looked like a hundred other girls in school, except for two things. She wore no makeup, and her eyes were the biggest I had ever seen, like deer's eyes caught in headlights. She twirled as she went past, her flaring skirt brushing my pant leg, and then she marched out of the lunchroom.

From among the tables came three slow claps. Someone whistled. Someone yelped.

Kevin and I gawked at each other.

Kevin held up his hands and framed a marquee[2] in the air. "*Hot Seat!* Coming Attraction—Stargirl!"

I slapped the table. "Yes!"

We slammed hands.

---

2. **marquee.** Movie theater sign

Chapter 2

When we got to school the next day, Hillari Kimble was holding court at the door.

"She's not real," Hillari said. She was sneering. "She's an actress. It's a scam."

Someone called out, "Who's scamming us?"

"The administration. The principal. Who else? Who cares?" Hillari wagged her head at the <u>absurdity</u> of the question.

◀ Who does Hillari believe is scamming the students?

A hand flashed in the air: "Why?"

"School spirit," she spat back. "They think this place was too dead last year. They think if they plant some nutcase in with the students—"

"Like they plant narcs[1] in schools!" someone else shouted.

Hillari glared at the speaker, then continued,

"—some nutcase who stirs things up, then maybe all the little students will go to a game once in a while or join a club."

"Instead of making out in the library!" chimed another voice. And everybody laughed and the bell rang and we went in.

Hillari Kimble's theory spread throughout the school and was widely accepted.

"You think Hillari's right?" Kevin asked me. "Stargirl's a plant?"

I snickered. "Listen to yourself."

He spread his arms. "What?"

"This is Mica Area High School," I reminded him. "It's not a CIA operation."

"Maybe not," he said, "but I hope Hillari's right."

"Why would you hope that? If she's not a real student, we can't have her on *Hot Seat*."

Kevin wagged his head and grinned. "As usual, Mr. Director, you fail to see the whole picture. We could use the show to expose her. Can't you see it?" He did

◀ What is Kevin's plan for exposing Stargirl?

---

1. **narcs.** People who investigate narcotics violations

words for everyday use   ab • surd (əb sərd') *n.*, something that is clearly ridiculous. *It was <u>absurd</u> to see a dog being pushed in a baby carriage.* **absurdity,** *adj.*

the marquee thing with this hands: *"Hot Seat Uncovers Faculty Hoax!"*

I stared at him. "You *want* her to be a fake, don't you?"

He grinned ear to ear. "Absolutely. Our ratings will go sky-high!"

I had to admit, the more I saw of her, the easier it was to believe she was a plant, a joke, anything but real. On that second day she wore bright-red baggy shorts with a bib and shoulder straps—overall shorts. Her sandy hair was pulled back into twin plaited pigtails,[2] each tied with a bright-red ribbon. A rouge smudge appled each cheek, and she had even dabbed some oversized freckles on her face. She looked like Heidi. Or Bo Peep.[3]

At lunch she was alone again at her table. As before, when she finished eating, she took up her ukulele. But this time she didn't play. She got up and started walking among the tables. She stared at us. She stared at one face, then another and another. The kind of bold, I'm-looking-at-you stare you almost never get from people, especially strangers. She appeared to be looking for someone, and the whole lunchroom had become very uncomfortable.

As she approached our table, I thought: *What if she's looking for me?* The thought terrified me. So I turned from her. I looked at Kevin. I watched him grin goofily up at her. He wiggled his fingers at her and whispered, "Hi, Stargirl." I didn't hear an answer. I was intensely aware of her passing behind my chair.

She stopped two tables away. She was smiling at a pudding-bodied senior named Alan Ferko. The lunchroom was dead silent. She started strumming the uke. And singing. It was "Happy Birthday." When she came to his name she didn't sing just his first name, but his full name:

"Happy Birthday, dear Alan Fer-kooooh"

▶ What does Stargirl sing in the lunchroom?

---

2. **twin plaited pigtails.** Hair braided into two braids
3. **She looked like Heidi. Or Bo Peep.** Heidi and Bo Peep are fictional story-book characters.

Alan Ferko's face turned red as Bo Peep's pigtail ribbons. There was a flurry of whistles and hoots, more for Alan Ferko's sake, I think, than hers. As Stargirl marched out, I could see Hillari Kimble across the lunchroom rising from her seat, pointing, saying something I could not hear.

"I'll tell you one thing," Kevin said as we joined the mob in the hallways, "she better be fake."

I asked him what he meant.

"I mean if she's real, she's in big trouble. How long do you think somebody who's *really* like that is going to last around here?"

Good question.

Mica Area High School—MAHS—was not exactly a hotbed of nonconformity. There were individual variants here and there, of course, but within pretty narrow limits we all wore the same clothes, talked the same way, ate the same food, listened to the same music. Even our dorks and nerds had a MAHS stamp on them. If we happened to somehow distinguish ourselves, we quickly snapped back into place, like rubber bands.

Kevin was right. It was unthinkable that Stargirl could survive—or at least survive unchanged—among us. But it was also clear that Hillari Kimble was at least half right: this person calling herself Stargirl may or may not have been a faculty plant for school spirit, but whatever she was, she was not real.

She couldn't be.

Several times in those early weeks of September, she showed up in something outrageous. A 1920s

---

words for everyday use

hot • bed (hät' bed) *n.*, environment that favors rapid growth or development. *The riverside neighborhood was a hotbed of crime.*

non • con • for • mi • ty (nän' kən fôr' mə tē) *n.*, refusal to conform to an established creed, rule, or practice. *My parents believe in nonconformity; my brothers and I have no curfew.*

var • i • ant (ver' ē ənt) *n.*, something that differs from the standard form. *Jennet's brightly colored sail appeared to be the only variant in the cluster of white-sailed boats.*

dis • tin • guish (di stin' gwish) *v.*, to discern; to detect with the eyes or with other senses. *I could not quite distinguish her face in the poorly-lit room, so I was not sure who she was.*

flapper dress.[4] An Indian buckskin.[5] A kimono.[6] One day she wore a denim miniskirt with green stockings, and crawling up one leg was a parade of enamel lady-bug and butterfly pins. "Normal" for her were long, floor-brushing pioneer dresses and skirts.

Every few days in the lunchroom she <u>serenaded</u> someone new with "Happy Birthday." I was glad my birthday was in the summer.

In the hallways, she said hello to perfect strangers. The seniors couldn't believe it. They had never seen a tenth-grader so bold.

In class she was always flapping her hand in the air, asking questions, though the question often had nothing to do with the subject. One day she asked a question about trolls—in U.S. History class.

She made up a song about isosceles triangles.[7] She sang it to her Plane Geometry class. It was called "Three Sides Have I, But Only Two Are Equal."

She joined the cross-country team. Our home meets were held on the Mica Country Club golf course. Red flags showed the runners the way to go. In her first meet, out in the middle of the course, she turned left when everyone else turned right. They waited for her at the finish line. She never showed up. She was dismissed from the team.

One day a girl screamed in the hallway. She had seen a tiny brown face pop up from Stargirl's sunflower canvas bag. It was her pet rat. It rode to school in the bag every day.

One morning we had a rare rainfall. It came during her gym glass. The teacher told everyone to come

► What is "normal" for Stargirl?

► What is the result of Stargirl turning left instead of right and never returning to her cross-country team?

---

4. **flapper dress.** Dress worn by flappers, or women that showed freedom from conventions in the 1920s. Flapper dresses were tank-top style with short skirts.

5. **Indian buckskin.** Clothing made out of the hides of deer, as worn by some early American Indians

6. **kimono.** Long robe with wide sleeves traditionally worn with a broad sash as an outer garment by the Japanese

7. **isosceles triangles.** A triangle having two equal sides

words for everyday use

ser • e • nade (ser' ə nād') v., perform a complimentary vocal or instrumental piece of music. *We were <u>serenaded</u> with lovely guitar music as we ate our lunch at the park.*

in. On the way to the next class they looked out the windows. Stargirl was still outside. In the rain. Dancing.

We wanted to define her, to wrap her up as we did each other, but we could not seem to get past "weird" and "strange" and "goofy." Her ways knocked us off balance. A single word seemed to <u>hover</u> in the cloudless sky over the school:

HUH?

Everything she did seemed to echo Hillari Kimble: She's not real . . . She's not real . . .

And each night in bed I thought of her as the moon came through my window. I could have lowered my shade to make it darker and easier to sleep, but I never did. In that moonlit hour, I <u>acquired</u> a sense of the otherness of things. I liked the feeling the moonlight gave me, as if it wasn't the opposite of day, but its underside, its private side, when the fabulous purred on my snow-white sheet like some dark cat come in from the desert.

It was during one of these nightmoon times that it came to me that Hillari Kimble was wrong. Stargirl *was* real.

words for everyday use

hov • er (hə' ver) v., stay suspended in the air near one place. *The helicopter <u>hovered</u> above the landing sight until the pilot was certain of a clear landing.*

ac • quire (ə kwir') v., get. *I <u>acquired</u> a new teapot to add to my growing collection.*

Chapter 3

We fought daily, Kevin and I.

My main job as producer was to <u>recruit</u> people for the Hot Seat. After I signed someone up, Kevin began researching the person, getting his questions ready:

Every day he asked me, "Did you sign her up?"

Every day I answered no.

He got frustrated.

"What do you mean, no? Don't you *want* to sign her up?"

I told him I wasn't sure.

His eyes bugged out. "Not sure? How can you not be sure? We high-fived in the lunchroom weeks ago. We were thinking Stargirl mini-series, even. This is a *Hot Seat* from heaven."

I shrugged. "That was then. Now I'm not sure."

He looked at me like I had three ears. "What's there to be not sure about?"

I shrugged.

"Well then," he said, "*I'll* sign her up." He walked away.

▶ What does Leo tell Kevin after Kevin says he'll sign Stargirl up for the show?

"You'll have to find another director, then," I said.

He stopped. I could almost see the steam rising from his shoulders. He turned, pointed. "Leo, you can be a real jerk sometimes." He walked off.

It was uncomfortable. Kevin Quinlan and I usually agreed on everything. We had been best friends since arriving in Arizona the same week four years before. We both thought the prickly pear cactus looked like Ping-Pong paddles with whiskers, and that saguaros[1] looked like dinosaur mittens. We both loved strawberry-banana smoothies. We both wanted to go into television. Kevin often said he wanted to be a sleazy talk show host, and he wasn't kidding. I wanted to be a sports announcer or news anchor. We conceived *Hot Seat* together and convinced the faculty to let us

▶ What does Kevin want to do for his career in the future?

---

1. **saguaros.** Kind of cactus found in southwestern U.S. and Mexico

words for everyday use   re • cruit (ri krüt') *v.*, enlist new members. *We have to <u>recruit</u> students to join chess club so that it won't have to disband due to lack of enrollment.*

do it. It was an instant hit. It quickly became the most popular thing in school.

So why was I balking?

I didn't know. I had some vague feelings, but the only one I could identify was a warning: Leave her alone.

In time "Hillari's Hypothesis" (so called by Kevin) about Stargirl's origins gave way to other theories.

She was trying to get herself discovered for the movies.

She was sniffing fumes.

She was homeschooling gone amok.

She was an alien.

The rat she brought to school was only the tip of the iceberg. She had hundreds of them at home, some as big as cats.

She lived in a ghost town in the desert.

She lived in a bus.

Her parents were circus acrobats.

Her parents were witches.

Her parents were brain-dead vegetables in a hospital in Yuma.

We watched her sit down in class and pull from her canvas bag a blue and yellow ruffled curtain that she draped over three sides of her desk. We saw her set out a three-inch clear glass vase and drop into it a white and yellow daisy. She did and undid this in every class she attended, six times a day. Only on Monday mornings was the daisy fresh. By last period the petals were drooping. By Wednesday the petals began to fall, the stem to sag. By Friday the flower hung down over the rim of the waterless vase, its dead stump of a head shedding yellow dust in the pencil groove.

◄ What does Stargirl's flower look like by Friday?

We joined her as she sang "Happy Birthday" to us in the lunchroom. We heard her greet us in the hallways and classrooms, and we wondered how she knew our names and our birthdays.

words for everyday use

balk (bòk') v., refuse abruptly. *My sister balked at loaning me her favorite blouse for the evening, so I chose a different one.*

vague (vāg') adj., not clearly expressed. *The teacher's vague instructions left me completely confused over the assignment.*

amok (ə mək') adv., undisciplined, uncontrolled, or faulty manner. *The students ran amok without the attention of their teacher.*

Her caught-in-headlights eyes gave her a look of perpetual astonishment, so that we found ourselves turning and looking back over our shoulders, wondering what we were missing.

She laughed when there was no joke. She danced when there was no music.

She had no friends, yet she was the friendliest person in school.

In her answers in class she often spoke of sea horses and stars, but she did not know what a football was.

She said there was no television in her house.

She was elusive. She was today. She was tomorrow. She was the faintest scent of a cactus flower, the flirting shadow of an elf owl. We did not know what to make of her. In our minds we tried to pin her to a corkboard like a butterfly, but the pin merely went through and away she flew.

* * *

Kevin wasn't the only one. Other kids pestered me: "Put her on the Hot Seat!"

I lied. I said she was only a tenth-grader and you had to be at least a junior to be on *Hot Seat.*

Meanwhile, I kept my distance. I observed her as if she were a bird in an aviary.[2] One day I turned a corner and there she was, coming right at me, the long skirt softly rustling, looking straight at me, surrounding me with those eyes. I turned and trotted off the other way. Seating myself in my next class, I felt warm, shaken. I wondered if my foolishness showed. Was I myself becoming goofy? The feeling I had had when I saw her around the corner had been something like panic.

Then one day after school I followed her. I kept at a safe distance. Since she was known not to take a bus, I expected the walk to be short. It wasn't. We

---

2. **aviary.** Place for keeping birds confined

trekked all over Mica, past hundreds of grassless stone-and-cactus front yards, through the Tudorized shopping center, skirting the electronics business park around which the city had been invented a mere fifteen years before.

At one point she pulled a piece of paper from her bag. She consulted it. She seemed to be reading house numbers as she walked along. Abruptly she turned up a driveway, went to the front door, and left something in the mailbox.

I waited for her to move off. I looked around—no one on the street. I went to the mailbox, pulled out a homemade card, opened it. Each tall letter was a different painted color. The card said: CONGRATULATIONS! It was unsigned.

◀ What does Leo find in the mailbox?

I <u>resumed</u> following her. Cars pulled into driveways. It was dinnertime. My parents would be wondering.

She took the rat from the bag and put it on her shoulder. Riding there, the rat faced backward, its tiny triangular face peeping out of her sand-colored hair. I could not see its beady black eyes, but I guessed it was looking at me. I fancied it was telling her what it saw. I fell farther back.

Shadows crossed the streets.

We passed the car wash and the bike shop. We passed the country club golf course, the biggest spread of green grass until the next golf course in the next town. We passed the "Welcome to Mica" sign. We were walking westward. There was us and the highway and the desert and the sun blazing above the Maricopa Mountains. I wished I had my sunglasses.

After a while she <u>veered</u> from the highway. I hesitated, then followed. She was walking directly into the setting sun, now a great orange perched atop the mountain crests. For a minute the mountains were the same dusky lavender as her sand-skimming skirt. With each step the silence grew, as did my sense that she knew—had known all along—that she was being

---

words for everyday use

re • sume (ri zōom´) v., take, get, or occupy again. *The performance was to resume after a short intermission.*

veer (vir´) v., change direction. *I veered away when I saw Stephanie coming down the hall, as I wasn't ready to talk to her.*

followed. Or more, that she was leading me. She never looked back.

She strummed her ukulele. She sang. I could no longer see the rat. I imagined it was dozing in the curtain of her hair. I imagined it was singing along. The sun lay down behind the mountains.

Where was she going?

In the gathering dusk, the saguaros flung shadows of giants across the pebbled earth. The air was cool on my face. The desert smelled of apples. I heard something—a coyote? I thought of rattlesnakes and scorpions.

I stopped. I watched her walk on. I <u>stifled</u> an impulse to call after her, to warn her . . . of what?

I turned and walked, then ran, back to the highway.

sti • fle (stī′ fəl) v., hold back, stop, smother. *It was hard to <u>stifle</u> my laughter while reading a comic book in the library.*

Chapter 4

At Mica Area High School, Hillari Kimble was famous for three things: her mouth, The Hoax, and Wayne Parr.

Her mouth spoke for itself, most often to complain.

The episode that became known as Hillari's Hoax took place in her sophomore year, when she tried out for cheerleading. Her face and hair and figure were right enough, and she surely had the mouth—she made the squad easily. And then she stunned everyone by turning it down. She said she just wanted to prove that she could do it. She said she had no intention of yammering and bouncing in front of empty bleachers (which was usually the case). And anyway, she hated sports.

◄ How does Hillari stun the other students after she makes the cheerleading squad?

As for Wayne Parr, he was her boyfriend. Mouthwise, he was her opposite: he seldom opened his. He didn't have to. All he had to do was appear. That was his job: appear. By both girls' and boys' standards, Wayne Parr was gorgeous.

But he was more—and less—than that.

In terms of achievement, Wayne Parr seemed to be nobody. He played on no sports team, joined no organization, won no awards, earned no A's. He was elected to nothing, honored for nothing—and yet, though I did not realize this until years later, he was grand marshal of our daily parade.

We did not wake up in the morning and ask ourselves, "What will Wayne Parr wear today?" or "How will Wayne Parr act today?" At least, not consciously. But on some level below awareness, that is exactly what we did. Wayne Parr did not go to football and basketball games, and by and large, neither did we. Wayne Parr did not ask questions in class or get worked up over teachers or pep rallies, and neither did we. Wayne Parr did not much care. Neither did we.

Did Parr create us, or was he simply a reflection of us? I didn't know. I knew only that if you peeled off one by one all the layers of the student body, you would have found at the core not the spirit of the school, but Wayne Parr. That's why, in our sophomore year, I had recruited Parr for the Hot Seat. Kevin was surprised.

"Why him?" Kevin said. "What's he ever done?"

What could I say? That Parr was a worthy subject precisely *because* he did nothing, *because* he was so <u>monumentally</u> good at doing nothing? I had only a vague insight, not the words. I just shrugged.

▶ Who is Parr's hero?

The highlight of that *Hot Seat* came when Kevin asked Parr who was his hero, his role model. It was one of Kevin's standard questions.

Parr answered, *"GQ."*

In the control room, I did a double take. Was the sound working right?

"*GQ?*" Kevin repeated dumbly. "*Gentleman's Quarterly?* The magazine?"

Parr did not look at Kevin. He looked straight at the camera. He nodded smugly. He went on to say he wanted to become a male model, his ultimate ambition was to be on the cover of *GQ*. And right there he posed for the camera—he had that <u>disdainful</u> model look down pat—and suddenly I could see it: the jaw square as the corner of a cover, the <u>chiseled</u> cheeks, the perfect teeth and hair.

That, as I say, took place toward the end of our sophomore year. I thought then that Wayne Parr would always reign as our grand marshal. How could I have known that he would soon be challenged by a freckle-nosed homeschooler?

---

words for everyday use

mon • u • men • tal (män′ yə men′ təl) *adj.*, outstanding; very great. *Winning the debate was more than good—it was monumental.* **monumentally,** *adv.*

dis • dain • ful (dis dān′ fəl) *adj.*, to be full of scorn or contempt. *His disdainful* attitude reflected his unhappiness at losing his job.

chis • eled (chi′ zəld) *adj.*, formed or crafted as if with a chisel. *His chiseled features were so pronounced that he looked like a walking sculpture.*

Chapter 5

The call came from Kevin on a Friday night. He was at the football game. "Quick! Hurry! Drop whatever you're doing! Now!"

Kevin was one of the few who went to games. The school kept threatening to drop football because of low attendance. They said ticket receipts were barely enough to pay for electricity to light the field.

◀ Why does the school threaten to drop the football team?

But Kevin was screaming on the phone. I jumped in the family pickup and raced to the stadium.

I bolted from the truck. Kevin was at the gate, windmilling his arm: "Hurry!" I threw the two dollar admission at the ticket window and we raced for the field. "See better up here," he said, yanking me into the stands. It was halftime. The band was on the field, all fourteen of them. Among the students it was known as "The World's Smallest Standing Band." There weren't enough of them to form recognizable letters or shapes—except for a capital "I"—so they didn't march much at halftimes of games. They mostly stood. In two rows of seven each, plus the student conductor. No majorettes.[1] No color guard.[2] No flag and rifle girls.[3]

Except this night. This night Stargirl Caraway was on the field with them. As they played, rooted in their places, she pranced around the grass in her bare feet and long lemon-yellow dress. She roamed from goalpost to goalpost. She swirled like a dust devil. She marched stiffly like a wooden soldier. She tootled an imaginary flute. She pogoed into the air[4] and knocked her bare heels together. The cheerleaders gaped from the sidelines. A few people in the stands whistled. The rest—they barely outnumbered the band—sat there with *What is this?* on their faces.

The band stopped playing and marched off the field. Stargirl stayed. She was twirling down the forty-yard line when the players returned. They did a minute of warm-up exercises. She joined in: jumping

◀ What does Stargirl do when the band marches off the field? How does the crowd react once she leaves the stadium?

---

1. **majorettes.** Baton twirlers who accompany a marching band
2. **color guard.** Honor guard for the colors of an organization
3. **flag and rifle girls.** Girls who perform precision routines with flags or rifles as part of a marching band
4. **pogoed into the air.** Jumped

jacks, belly whomps.[5] The teams lined up for the second half kickoff. The ball perched on the kicking tee. She was still on the field. The referee blew his whistle, pointed to her. He flapped his hand for her to go away. Instead, she dashed for the ball. She plucked it off the tee and danced with it, spinning and hugging it and hoisting it into the air. The players looked at their coaches. The coaches looked at the officials. The officials blew their whistles and began <u>converging</u> on her. The sole policeman on duty headed for the field. She punted the ball over the visiting team's bench and ran from the field and out of the stadium.

Everyone cheered: the spectators, the cheerleaders, the band, the players, the officials, the parents running the hot dog stand, the policeman, me. We whistled and stomped our feet on the aluminum bleachers. The cheerleaders stared up in delighted surprise. For the first time, they were hearing something come back from the stands. They did cartwheels and backflips and even a three-tier pyramid. Old-timers—or as old as timers got in a city as young as Mica—said they had never heard such a racket.

* * *

▶ Who does not show up for the next home game?

For the next home game more than a thousand people showed up. Everyone but Wayne Parr and Hillari Kimble. There was a line at the ticket window. The refreshment stand ran out of hot dogs. A second policeman was called in. The cheerleaders were in their glory. They screamed up at the bleachers: "GIMME AN E!" The bleachers screamed back: "EEEE!" (We were the Electrons, in honor of the town's electronics heritage.)

The cheerleaders ran through all their routines before the first quarter was over. The band was loud and peppy. The football team even scored a touch-

---

5. **belly whomps.** Exercises in which players alternately run in place and lower themselves to the ground in pushup form

words for everyday use   con • verge (kən vʉrj´) vi., come together. *The two small streams <u>converged</u> into a mighty river.*

down. In the stands heads kept swinging to the edges of the field, to the entrance, to the streetlamp-lighted darkness behind the stadium. The sense of <u>expectation</u> grew as the first half came to a close. The band marched smartly onto the field. Even they were looking around.

The musicians did their program. They even formed a small, lopsided circle. They seemed to linger on the field, drawing out their notes, waiting. Finally, <u>reluctantly</u>, they marched to the sideline. The players returned. They kept glancing around as they did their warm-ups. When the referee raised his arm and blew his whistle for the second half to begin, a sense of disappointment fell over the stadium. The cheerleaders' shoulders sagged.

She wasn't coming.

* * *

On the following Monday, we got a shock in the lunchroom. Bleached blond and beautiful Mallory Stillwell, captain of the cheerleaders, was sitting with Stargirl. She sat with her, ate with her, talked with her, walked out with her. By sixth period the whole school knew: Stargirl had been invited to become a cheerleader and had said yes.

◀ How does Stargirl respond to being asked to join the cheerleading squad?

People in Phoenix must have heard us buzzing. Would she wear the usual skirt and sweater like everyone else? Would she do the usual cheers? Did all the cheerleaders want this, or was it just the captain's idea? Were they jealous?

Cheerleading practice drew a crowd. At least a hundred of us stood by the parking lot that day, watching her learn the cheers, watching her jump around in her long pioneer dress.

She spent two weeks practicing. Halfway through the second week she wore her uniform: green-trimmed white V-neck cotton sweater, short green and white pleated skirt. She looked just like the rest of them.

words for everyday use

ex • pec • ta • tion (ek spek tā shən) *n.*, anticipation. *My <u>expectations</u> grew as I waited for the performance to begin.*

re • luc • tant (ri lək' tənt) *adj.*, not in the mood, disinclined. *I didn't understand why my brother was <u>reluctant</u> to go to the movie, but after seeing it, I understood.*

▶ What do the students find on their desks on Halloween?

Still, to us she was not truly a cheerleader, but Stargirl dressed like one. She continued to strum her ukulele and sing "Happy Birthday" to people. She still wore long skirts on non-game days and made a home of her school desks. When Halloween arrived, everyone in her homeroom found a candy pumpkin on his or her desk. No one had to ask who did it. By then most of us had decided that we liked having her around. We found ourselves looking forward to coming to school, to seeing what <u>bizarre</u> <u>antic</u> she'd be up to. She gave us something to talk about. She was entertaining.

At the same time, we held back. Because she was different. *Different.* We had no one to compare her to, no one to measure her against. She was unknown territory. Unsafe. We were afraid to get too close.

▶ Whose birthday is coming up next?

Also, I think we were all waiting to see the outcome of an event that loomed larger and larger with every passing day. The next birthday coming up was Hillari Kimble's.

---

words for everyday use

bi • zarre (bə zär') *adj.,* strikingly out of the ordinary. *Phillip was acting so bizarre during class that the teacher asked him to leave.*

an • tic (an' tik) *n.,* attention-drawing act or action. *Her unusual antic during the ceremony did not win the sympathies of the guests.*

Chapter 6

Hillari herself set the stage the day before. In the middle of lunch, she got up from her table and walked over to Stargirl. For half a minute she just stood behind Stargirl's chair. Silence everywhere except for tinklings in the kitchen. Only Stargirl was still chewing. Hillari moved around to the side.

I'm Hillari Kimble," she said.

Stargirl looked up. She smiled. She said, "I know."

"My birthday is tomorrow."

"I know."

Hillari paused. Her eyes narrowed. She jabbed her finger in Stargirl's face. "Don't try singing to me, I'm warning you."

◀ What does Hillari tell Stargirl in the lunchroom?

Only those at nearby tables heard Stargirl's faint reply: "I won't sing to you."

Hillari gave a satisfied smirk and walked off.

From the moment we arrived at school the next day, the atmosphere bristled like cactus paddles. When the buzzer sounded for first lunch, we leaped for the doors. We swarmed into the food lines. We raced through our choices and hurried to our seats. Never had we moved so fast so quietly. At most, we whispered. We sat, we ate. We were afraid to crunch our potato chips, afraid we might miss something.

Hillari was first to enter. She marched in, leading her girlfriends like an invading general. In the food line, she smacked items onto her tray. She glared at the cashier. While her friends scanned the crowd for Stargirl, Hillari stared ferociously at her sandwich.

Wayne Parr came in and sat several tables away, as if even he was afraid of her on this day.

◀ Who sits several tables away from Hillari in the lunchroom?

Stargirl finally came in. She went straight to the food line <u>blithely</u> smiling as usual. Both she and Hillari seemed unaware of each other.

Stargirl ate. Hillari ate. We watched. Only the clock moved.

---

words for everyday use   **blithe** (blīth′) adj., cheerful, carefree. *The girl offered a <u>blithe</u> smile when the waitress brought her the ice cream.* **blithely,** adv.

A kitchen staffer stuck her head out over the conveyor belt and called: "Trays!"

A voice barked back: "Shut up!"

Stargirl finished her lunch. As usual, she stuffed her wrappings into her paper bag, carried the bag to the paper-only can by the tray return window, and dropped it in. She returned to her seat. She picked up the ukulele. We stopped breathing. Hillari stared at her sandwich.

Stargirl began strumming and humming. She stood. She strolled between the tables, humming, strumming. Three hundred pairs of eyes followed her. She came to Hillari Kimble's table—and kept on walking, right up to the table where Kevin and I sat with the *Hot Seat* crew. She stopped and she sang "Happy Birthday." It was Hillari's name at the end of the song, but true to her word of the day before, she did not sing it *to* Hillari—she sang it to me. She stood at my shoulder and looked down at me, smiling and singing, and I didn't know whether to look down at my hands or up at her face, so I did some of each. My face was burning.

When she finished, the students burst from their silence with wild applause. Hillari Kimble stomped from the lunchroom. Kevin looked up at Stargirl and pointed at me and said what everyone must have been thinking: "Why him?"

▶ What is Stargirl's response to Kevin's question of "Why him?"

Stargirl tilted her head, as if studying me. She grinned <u>mischievously</u>. She tugged on my earlobe and said, "He's cute." And walked off.

I was feeling nine ways at once, and they all ended up at the touch of her hand on my ear—until Kevin reached over and yanked the same earlobe. "This keeps getting more interesting," he said. "I think it's time to go see Archie."

---

words for everyday use
mis • chie • vous (mis′ chə vəs) *adj.*, irresponsibly playful. *I knew from her <u>mischievous</u> smile that she planned to disobey the instructions.* **mischievously,** *adv.*

Chapter 7

A. H. (Archibald Hapwood) Brubaker lived in a house of bones. Jawbones, hipbones, femurs. There were bones in every room, every closet, on the back porch. Some people have stone cats on their roofs; on his roof Archie Brubaker had a skeleton of Monroe, his deceased Siamese. Take a seat in his bathroom and you found yourself facing the faintly smirking skull of Doris, a prehistoric creodont.[1] Open the kitchen cabinet where the peanut butter was kept and you were face to fossil face with an extinct fox.

Archie was not <u>morbid</u>; he was a paleontologist.[2] The bones were from digs he had done throughout the American West. Many were rightly his, found in his spare time. Others he collected for museums but slipped into his own pocket or knapsack instead. "Better to sit in my refrigerator than disappear in a drawer in some museum basement," he would say.

When he wasn't digging up old bones, Archie Brubaker was teaching at universities in the East. He retired at the age of sixty-five. When he was sixty-six, his wife, Ada Mae, died. At sixty-seven he moved himself and his bones west, "to join the other fossils."

◀ What does Archie do when he's not digging up old bones?

He chose his home for two reasons: (1) its proximity to the high school (he wanted to be near kids; he had none of his own) and (2) "Señor Saguaro." Señor Saguaro was a cactus, a thirty-foot-tall giant that towered over the toolshed in the backyard. It had two arms high on the trunk. One stuck straight out; the other made a right turn upward, as if waving "adiós!"[3] The waving arm was green from the elbow up; all else was brown, dead. Much of the thick, leathery skin along the trunk had come loose and crumpled in a heap about the massive foot: Señor

---

1. **creodont.** Small, primitive, flesh-eating mammal
2. **paleontologist.** Person who studies fossils
3. **"adiós."** Spanish word for *goodbye*

---

words for everyday use   mor • bid (môr′ bəd) *adj.*, abnormally susceptible to or characterized by gloomy or unwholesome feelings. *I didn't want to hear the <u>morbid</u> tales of detective work.*

Saguaro had lost his pants. Only his ribs, thumb-thick vertical timbers, held him up. Elf owls nested in his chest.

The old professor often talked to Señor Saguaro—and to us. He was not certified to teach in Arizona, but that did not stop him. Every Saturday morning his house became a school. Fourth-graders, twelfth-graders—all were welcome. No tests, no grades, no attendance record. Just the best school most of us had ever gone to. He covered everything from tooth-paste to tapeworms and somehow made it all fit together. He called us the Loyal Order of the Stone Bone. He gave us homemade necklaces. The pendant was a small fossil bone strung on rawhide. Years before, he had told his first class, "Call me Archie." He never had to say it again.

After dinner that day, Kevin and I walked over to Archie's. Though the official class <u>convened</u> on Saturday morning, kids were welcome anytime. "My school," he said, "is everywhere and always in session."

We found him, as usual, on the back porch, rocking and reading. The porch, bathed in the red-gold light of sunset, faced the Maricopas. Archie's white hair seemed to give off a light of its own.

The moment he saw us, he put down his book. "Students! Welcome!"

"Archie," we said, then turned to greet the great cactus, as visitors were expected to do: "Señor Saguaro." We saluted.

We sat on rockers; the porch was full of them. "So, men," he said, "business or pleasure?"

"<u>Bafflement</u>," I said. "There's a new girl in school."

He laughed. "Stargirl."

Kevin's eyes popped. "You know her?"

"Know her?" he said. He picked up his pipe and loaded it with cherrysweet tobacco. He always did this when settling in for a long lecture or conversation. "Good question." He lit the pipe. "Let's say she's been

▶ *What happens at Archie's house every Saturday morning?*

---

words for everyday use

con • vene (kən vēn') vi., come together in a body. *The meeting <u>convened</u> every Monday morning at ten o'clock.*

baf • fle • ment (ba' fəl ment) n., confusing or puzzling. *He was in complete <u>bafflement</u> over who this new girl was trying to be.*

on the porch here quite a few times." White smoke puffed like Apache signals from the corner of his mouth. "I was wondering when you'd start asking questions." He chuckled to himself. "Bafflement . . . good word. She *is* different, isn't she?"

Kevin and I burst into laughter and nods. At that moment I realized how much I had been craving Archie's confirmation.

Kevin exclaimed, "Like another species!"

Archie cocked his head, as if he had just caught the sound of a rare bird. The pipe stem anchored a <u>wry</u> grin. A sweet scent filled the air about our rocking chairs. He stared at Kevin. "On the <u>contrary</u>, she is one of us. Most decidedly. She is us more than we are us. She is, I think, who we really are. Or were."

Archie talked that way sometimes, in riddles. We didn't always know what he was saying, but our ears didn't much care. We just wanted to hear more. As the sun dipped below the mountains, it fired a final dart at Archie's flashing eyebrows.

"She's homeschooled, you know. Her mother brought her to me. I guess she wanted a break from playing teacher. One day a week. Four, five—yes, five years now."

Kevin pointed. "You created her!"

Archie smiled, puffed. "No, that was done long before me."

"Some people are saying she's some kind of alien sent down here from Alpha Centauri[4] or something," said Kevin. He chuckled, but not too convincingly. He half believed it.

Archie's pipe had gone out. He relit it. "She's anything but. She's an earthling if there ever was one."

"So it's not just an act?" said Kevin.

"An act? No. If anybody is acting, it's us. She's as real as"—he looked around; he picked up the tiny,

◀ What does Leo realize he's been craving?

◀ How long has Stargirl been coming to Archie's house?

---

4. **Alpha Centauri**. Star nearest the earth

| words for everyday use | wry (rī) *adj.*, ironic or sarcastic; grimly humorous. *After her <u>wry</u> comment, I knew I shouldn't take her seriously.* | con • trary (kän' trer ē) *adj.*, opposite. *<u>Contrary</u> to my parents' wishes, I decided to dye my hair blue.* |

wedgelike skull of Barney, a 60-million-year-old Paleocene[5] rodent, and held it up—"as real as Barney."

I felt a little jolt of pride at having reached this conclusion myself.

"But the name," said Kevin, leaning forward. "Is it real?"

"The name?" Archie shrugged. "Every name is real. That's the nature of names. When she first showed up, she called herself Pocket Mouse. Then Mudpie. Then—what?—Hullygully, I believe. Now . . ."

▶ What were Stargirl's names before Stargirl?

"Stargirl." The word came out whispery; my throat was dry.

Archie looked at me. "Whatever strikes her fancy. Maybe that's how names ought to be, heh? Why be stuck with just one your whole life?"

"What about her parents?" said Kevin.

"What about them?"

"What do they think?"

Archie shrugged. "I guess they agree."

"What do they do?" Kevin said.

"Breathe. Eat. Clip their toenails."

Kevin laughed. "You know what I mean. Where do they work?"

"Mrs. Caraway, until a few months ago, was Stargirl's teacher. I understand she also makes costumes for movies."

Kevin poked me. "The crazy clothes!"

▶ Where does Stargirl's father work?

"Her father, Charles, works—" he smiled at us "where else?"

"MicaTronics," we said in chorus.

I said it with wonder, for I had imagined something more <u>exotic</u>.

Kevin said, "So where is she from?"

---

5. **Paleocene**. Relating to the earliest epoch of the Tertiary or the corresponding system of rocks; period of great development of primitive mammals

---

words for everyday use   ex • ot • ic (ek so′ tik) *adj.,* not native to the place where found; foreign; exciting or mysterious. *The <u>exotic</u> woman, wearing a veil and cloak, was easy to spot.*

A natural question in a city as young as Mica. Nearly everybody had been born somewhere else.

Archie's eyebrows went up. "Good question." He took a long pull on the pipe. "Some would say Minnesota, but in her case . . ." He let out the smoke, his face disappearing in a gray cloud. A sweet haze veiled the sunset: cherries roasting in the Maricopas. He whispered, "Rara avis."[6]

"Archie," said Kevin, "you're not making a lot of sense."

Archie laughed, "Do I ever?"

Kevin jumped up. "I want to put her on *Hot Seat*. Dorko Borlock here doesn't want to."

Archie studied me through the smoke. I thought I saw approval, but when he spoke, he merely said, "Work it out, men."

We talked until dark. We said "adiós" to Señor Saguaro. On our way out, Archie said, more to me than to Kevin, I thought: "You'll know her more by your questions than by her answers. Keep looking at her long enough. One day you might see someone you know."

◀ *What is Archie's response to Kevin and Leo's argument about having Stargirl on* Hot Seat?

---

6. **Rara avis.** An unusual or extraordinary person or thing; rarity; literally, "strange bird"

Respond to the Selection

Leo and Kevin have opposite views on whether or not to put Stargirl on *Hot Seat*. Predict what you think they will decide and what could result from that decision.

Investigate, Inquire, and Imagine

Recall: GATHERING FACTS

1a. What two things are different about Stargirl's face from the faces of other girls at school?

2a. At the second home football game, how did the cheerleaders and musicians perform during the first half of the game? Who did they expect to show up during the game?

3a. To whom does Stargirl look at while singing "Happy Birthday" to Hillari? How does it make this person feel?

Interpret: FINDING MEANING

1b. What might these traits suggest about Stargirl's personality and/or character?

2b. How do the cheerleaders react when they realize this person is not coming to the game? What influence did this person have over the people's response to the game?

3b. Why does this person feel this way?

Analyze: TAKING THINGS APART

4a. List the things about Stargirl that make her stand out from other students at Mica Area High School.

Synthesize: BRINGING THINGS TOGETHER

4b. What do these differences mean to the other students at Mica Area High School? Do they embrace her differences or reject them? Do you think the students' view of Stargirl is going to change in the story? If so, how?

Evaluate: MAKING JUDGMENTS

5a. Evaluate the students' reactions to Stargirl. Did you find their reactions to her believable? Why, or why not? Which student(s), if any, do you think could become a close friend(s) to Stargirl? Why?

Extend: CONNECTING IDEAS

5b. Do you think you'd try to become friends with Stargirl? Why, or why not? What kinds of judgments do you make when you meet someone for the first time?

Understanding Literature

NARRATOR. A **narrator** is a person or character who tells a story. Works of fiction almost always use a narrator. The narrator in a work of fiction may be a major or minor character or simply someone who witnessed or heard about the events being related. Who is the narrator of *Stargirl?*

FLASHBACK AND FORESHADOWING. A **flashback** is a part of a story, poem, or play that presents events that happened at an earlier time. **Foreshadowing** is the act of hinting at events that will happen later in a poem, story, or play. What information does the flashback in *Stargirl* provide? Find an example of foreshadowing in the flashback.

SIMILE. A **simile** is a comparison using *like* or *as*. What simile is used to describe the atmosphere at school at the beginning of Chapter 6? What is the meaning of this comparison?

Chapter 8

▶ What happened to Stargirl by December?

The change began around Thanksgiving. By December first, Stargirl Caraway had become the most popular person in school.

How did it happen?

Was it the cheerleading?

The last football game of the season was her first as a cheerleader. The grandstand was packed: students, parents, alumni. Never had so many people come to a football game to see a cheerleader.

She did all the regular cheers and routines. And more. In fact, she never stopped cheering. While the other girls were taking breaks, she went on jumping and yelling. She roamed. Areas that had always been ignored—the far ends of the grandstand, the spectators behind the goalposts, the snack bar parents—found themselves with their own arm-pumping cheerleader.

She ran straight across the fifty-yard line and joined the other team's cheerleaders. We laughed as they stood there with their mouths open. She cheered in front of the players' bench and was shooed away by a coach. At halftime she played her ukulele with the band.

In the second half she got acrobatic. She did cartwheels and backflips. At one point the game was stopped and three zebra-striped officials ran toward one end zone. She had shinnied[1] up a goalpost, tightrope-walked out to the middle of the crossbar, and was now standing there with her arms raised in a touchdown sign. She was commanded down, to a standing ovation and flashing cameras.

As we filed out afterward, no one mentioned how boring the game itself had been. No one cared that the Electrons had lost again. In his column next day, the sports editor of the *Mica Times* referred to her as "the best athlete on the field." We couldn't wait for basketball season.

Was it a Hillari Kimble backlash?

---

1. **shinnied.** Climbed, using both hands and legs for gripping

Several days after the birthday song, I heard a shout down the hallway: "Don't!" I ran. A crowd was gathered at the top of a stairwell. They were all staring at something. I pushed my way through. Hillari Kimble was standing at the upper landing, grinning. She was holding Cinnamon the rat, dangling by its tail over the railing, nothing but space between it and the first floor. Stargirl was on the steps below, looking up.

◀ What was Hillari about to do to Cinnamon?

The scene froze. The bell for the next class rang. Nobody moved. Stargirl said nothing, merely looked. The eight toes of Cinnamon's front paws splayed apart. Its tiny unblinking eyes were bulging, black as cloves. Again a voice rang out: "Don't, Hillari!" Suddenly Hillari dropped it. Someone screamed, but the rat fell only to the floor at Hillari's feet. She sent Stargirl a final sneer and left.

Was it Dori Dilson?

Dori Dilson was a brown-haired ninth-grader who wrote poems in a looseleaf notebook half as big as herself and whose name nobody knew until the day she sat down at Stargirl's table for lunch. Next day the table was full. No longer did Stargirl eat lunch— or walk the hallways or do anything else at school— alone.

Was it us?

Did we change? Why didn't Hillari Kimble drop the rat to its death? Did she see something in our eyes?

Whatever the reason, by the time we returned from Thanksgiving break, it was clear that the change had occurred. Suddenly Stargirl was not dangerous, and we rushed to embrace her. Calls of "Stargirl!" flew down the hallways. We couldn't say her name often enough. It tickled us to mention her name to strangers and watch the expressions on their faces.

words for everyday use   splay (splā') v., spread outward. *I splayed on the blanket, stretching my limbs in each direction.*

▶ How did the
students of MAHS
honor Stargirl?

Girls liked her. Boys liked her. And—most remarkable—the attention came from all kinds of kids: shy mice and princesses, jocks and eggheads.

We honored her by imitation. A chorus of ukuleles strummed in the lunchroom. Flowers appeared on classroom desks. One day it rained and a dozen girls ran outside to dance. The pet shop at the Mica Mall ran out of rats.

The best chance for us to express our admiration came in the first week of December. We were gathered in the auditorium for the annual <u>oratorical</u> contest. Sponsored by the Arizona League of Women Voters, the event was open to any high school student who cared to show his or her stuff as a public speaker. The microphone was yours for seven minutes. Talk about anything you like. The winner would move on to the district competition.

Usually only four or five students entered the contest at MAHS. That year there were thirteen, including Stargirl. You didn't have to be a judge to see that she was far and away the best. She gave an animated speech—a performance, really—titled "Elf Owl, Call Me by My First Name." Her gray-brown homesteader's dress was the color of her subject. I couldn't see her freckles from the audience, but I imagined them dancing on her nose as she flicked her head this way and that. When she finished, we stomped on the floor and whistled and shouted for more.

▶ How did the
students at Yuma
High react to their
fellow student's
winning of the
oratorical contest?

While the judges went through the <u>charade</u> of <u>conferring</u>, a film was shown. It was a brief documentary about the previous year's state finals. It featured the winner, a boy from Yuma. The most <u>riveting</u> moments of the film came not during the contest, but during its aftermath. When the boy arrived back at Yuma High, the whole school mobbed him in the

---

**words
for
everyday
use**

or • a • tor • i • cal (ôr ə tôr' i kəl) adj., relating to one distinguished for skill and power as a public speaker. After participating on the debate team for three years, I decided to partake in an <u>oratorical</u> contest.

cha • rade (shə rād') n., empty or deceptive act. I felt her apology was merely a <u>charade</u> and I did not accept it.

con • fer (kən fər') v., compare views. After watching the skater perform, the judges <u>conferred</u> for ten minutes before announcing their score.

riv • et • ing (ri' və tiŋ) adj., engrossing, fascinating. The students sat in complete silence, hanging on every word the teacher said in her <u>riveting</u> lecture.

parking lot: banners, cheerleaders, band music, confetti, streamers. Pumping his arms in the air, the returning hero rode their shoulders into school.

The film ended, the lights went on, and the judges proclaimed Stargirl the winner. She would now go on to the district competition in Red Rock, they said. The state finals would be held in Phoenix in April. Again and again we whooped and whistled.

Such was the <u>acclamation</u> we gave her in those last weeks of the year. But we also gave something to ourselves.

---

words for everyday use ac • clam • a • tion (a klə māʹ shən) *n.*, overwhelming affirmative vote by cheers, shouts, or applause. *When the performance ended, the audience gave forth a great <u>acclamation</u>, demanding an encore.*

Chapter 9

In the Sonoran Desert there are ponds. You could be standing in the middle of one and not know it, because the ponds are usually dry. Nor would you know that inches below your feet, frogs are sleeping, their heartbeats down to once or twice per minute. They lie <u>dormant</u> and waiting, these mud frogs, for without water their lives are incomplete, they are not fully themselves. For many months they sleep like this within the earth. And then the rain comes. And a hundred pairs of eyes pop out of the mud, and at night a hundred voices call across the moonlit water.

It was wonderful to see, wonderful to be in the middle of: we mud frogs awakening all around. We were awash in tiny attentions. Small gestures, words, <u>empathies</u> thought to be extinct came to life. For years the strangers among us had passed <u>sullenly</u> in the hallways; now we looked, we nodded, we smiled. If someone got an A, others celebrated, too. If someone sprained an ankle, others felt the pain. We discovered the color of each other's eyes.

It was a rebellion she led, a rebellion *for* rather than against. For ourselves. For the dormant mud frogs we had been for so long.

▶ How much newspaper space did the "Letters to the Editor" take up in the December edition?

Kids whose voices had never been heard before spoke up in class. "Letters to the Editor" filled a whole page of the school newspaper's December edition. More than a hundred students tried out for the Spring Revue. One kid started a camera club. Another wore Hush Puppies instead of sneakers. A plain, timid girl painted her toenails kelly green. A boy showed up with purple hair.

None of this was publicly acknowledged. There were no PA announcements, no TV coverage, no headlines in the *Mica Times:*

---

words for everyday use

dor • mant (dôr′ mənt) *adj.,* inoperative; inactive. *The hibernating bear lay <u>dormant</u> all winter.*

em • pa • thy (em′ pə thē) *n.,* ability to share in another's emotions. *I had great <u>empathy</u> for my brother as I listened to his explanation of missing the bus.*

sul • len (sə′ lən) *adj.,* gloomy, somber. *After losing the championship game, the teammates looked <u>sullen</u>.* **sullenly,** *adv.*

MAHS STUDENTS ASTIR
INDIVIDUALITY ERUPTS

But it was there; it was happening. I was used to peering through the lens, to framing the picture, and I could see it. I could feel it in myself. I felt lighter, <u>unshackled</u>, as if something I had been carrying had fallen away. But I didn't know what to do about it. There was no direction to my <u>liberation</u>. I had no urge to color my hair or trash my sneakers. So I just enjoyed the feeling and watched the once <u>amorphous</u> student body separate itself into hundreds of individuals. The pronoun "we" itself seemed to crack and drift apart in pieces.

Ironically, as we discovered and distinguished ourselves, a new collective came into being—a <u>vitality</u>, a presence, a spirit that had not been there before. It echoed from the rafters in the gym: "GO, ELECTRONS!" It sparkled in the water fountains. At the holiday assembly, the words of the alma mater[1] had wings.

"It's a miracle!" I gushed to Archie one day.

He stood on the edge of his back porch. He did not turn. He pulled the pipe slowly from between his lips. He spoke as if to Señor Saguaro or to the blazing mountains beyond.

"Best hope it's not," he said. "The trouble with miracles is, they don't last long."

◀ *What is the trouble with miracles?*

And the trouble with bad times is, you can't sleep through them.

It was a golden age, those few weeks in December and January. How could I know that when the end came, I would be in the middle of it?

---

1. **alma mater**. Song of a school, college, or university

---

words for everyday use

un • shack • le (ən shaˈ kəl) *v.*, free from shackles. *After years of feeling weighed down with my secret, I felt unshackled and alive after revealing it.*

lib • er • a • tion (li bə rāˈ shən) *n.*, act of setting free. *Once our liberation sunk in, we celebrated our freedom.*

amor • phous (ə mòrˈ fəs) *adj.*, having no definite form. *At the beginning of the year,* our *amorphous* cheerleading squad looked dreadful; but by the end of the year, they'd really pulled it together.

vi • tal • i • ty (vī talˈ ə tē) *n.*, energy; life. *I came home from my week at the spa with so much vitality that I was finally able to start back in with my hobbies.*

Chapter 10

All my resistance to putting Stargirl on *Hot Seat* vanished. "Okay," I said to Kevin, "let's do it. Schedule her." He started off. I grabbed his arm. "Wait—ask her first."

He laughed. "Right. Like she's gonna say no."

No one had ever said no to the Hot Seat. Any <u>reluctance</u> to answering personal or embarrassing questions always yielded to the <u>lure</u> of appearing on TV. If anyone could resist that lure, I figured it would be Stargirl. That day after school, Kevin came at me thumbs-up and grinning: "It's a go! She said yes!"

First I was surprised. This didn't fit my impression of her. I didn't know that this was an early glimpse of something I was soon to see much more of: behind the dazzling talents and differentness, she was far more normal than I had realized.

Then I was <u>elated</u>. We yipped. We high-fived. We saw visions of our most popular show ever.

This was mid-January. We set a date of February thirteenth, the day before Valentine's. We wanted a full month for buildup. With my resistance now gone, I jumped in with both feet. We planned a promo campaign. We got art students to do posters. We jotted down questions for Kevin to ask in case the jury ran out—fat chance of that happening. We didn't have to post the usual jury notice: dozens of kids volunteered.

And then things changed again.

* * *

In the courtyard of our school stood a five-foot sheet of plywood in the shape of a roadrunner. It was a bulletin board, strictly for student use, always taped and tacked with messages and announcements. One day we found the following computer printout taped to the plywood roadrunner:

▶ *What did Leo learn about Stargirl behind her talents and differentness?*

▶ *What did the students find taped to the roadrunner?*

---

words for everyday use

re • luc • tance (ri lək′ tən(t)s) *n.*, unwillingness. *The mother's <u>reluctance</u> to let her son attend the concert stemmed from a fear of peer pressure.*

lure (loor′) *n.*, temptation. *The <u>lure</u> of my favorite television show was strong, but I did my homework instead.*

elat • ed (ē lāt′ ed) *adj.*, filled with joy. *Upon seeing my name in first place at my hardest track event, I felt <u>elated</u>.*

"I pledge allegiance to the United Turtles of America and to the fruit bats of Borneo, one planet in the Milky Way, incredible, with justice and black bean burritos for all."

Handwritten across the bottom were the words: "This is how she says the Pledge of Allegiance."

No one had to tell us who "she" was. Apparently, she was overheard in homeroom as we said the Pledge each morning.

As far as I knew, we were not a particularly patriotic bunch. I didn't hear people saying they were offended. Some thought it was funny. Some giggled and nodded knowingly, as if to say, There she goes again. On the following mornings, more than one kid was heard reciting the new "pledge."

Within days a new story wildfired through the student body. A senior girl, Anna Grisdale, lost her grandfather after a long illness. The funeral took place on a Saturday morning. For a while everything seemed routine: the crowd of people at the church, the line of cars with their headlights on, the smaller group clustered around the grave for the final farewell. After the brief graveside service, the funeral director handed everyone a long-stemmed flower. Upon leaving, each mourner laid his or her flower over the casket. This was when Anna Grisdale first noticed Stargirl.

◀ When did Anna first notice Stargirl?

Through her own tears Anna could see that Stargirl was crying also. She wondered if Stargirl had been at the church as well. Even more, she wondered why Stargirl was there at all. Could she have been friends with her grandfather without Anna's knowing it? Anna's mother asked her who the unfamiliar girl was.

Afterward, the mourners were invited to Anna's house for lunch. About thirty came. There was a buffet of cold cuts and salads and cookies. Stargirl was there, chatting with members of the family but not eating or drinking anything.

Suddenly Anna heard her mother's voice. It was no louder than the others, but it was different: "What are you doing here?"

Sudden stillness. Everyone staring.

They were in front of the picture window. Anna had never seen her mother so angry. Mrs. Grisdale had been very close to her father. They had built an addition to their house so he could live with them.

She glared down at Stargirl. "Answer me."

Stargirl gave no reply. "You didn't even know him, did you?"

Still Stargirl said nothing.

"*Did* you?"

And then Anna's mother was flinging open the front door and pointing, as if <u>banishing</u> her to the desert. "Leave my house."

Stargirl left.

Danny Pike was nine years old. He loved to ride the bicycle he had gotten for his birthday. One day after school he lost control and plowed into a mailbox. He broke his leg, but that wasn't the worst of it. A blood clot developed. He was airlifted to Children's Hospital in Phoenix, where he was operated on. For a while it was touch and go, but within a week he was on his way back home.

All this was reported to the *Mica Times*. As was the celebration when Danny arrived at his home on Piñon Lane. The five-column photo in the *Times* showed Danny on his father's shoulders, surrounded by a mob of neighbors. In the foreground was a new bike, and a big sign that read:

WELCOME HOME, DANNY

It wasn't until days later that the front-page photo appeared on the plywood roadrunner. We gathered around to see something we hadn't noticed before. An arrow from a thick red felt-tip marker pointed at one of the tiny faces crowded into the frame. It was the face of a girl, beaming as if Danny Pike were her little brother back from the dead. It was Stargirl.

▶ *To whose face was the arrow pointing?*

---

words for everyday use   **ban • ish** (ba′ nish) *v.*, drive out or remove from a place. *After the hoodlums messed up the restaurant, they were <u>banished</u> from ever returning.*

And then there was the bike.

The various members of the Pike family—parents, grandparents, et al.—each thought someone else had bought Danny the new bicycle. Several days went by before they discovered to their great surprise that none of them had.

So where did the bike come from? High-schoolers who heard the story and saw the picture had a pretty good idea. Apparently the Pikes did not. The bike became the focus of a family squabble. Mr. Pike was mad because nobody he asked would admit to buying the bike—and probably because he hadn't done it himself. Mrs. Pike was mad because no way, not for at least one year, would she allow Danny back on wheels.

One night the new, still-unridden bike wound up at the Pikes' front curb with the trash cans. By the time the trash collector came the next day, it was gone. Danny got a BB gun instead.

The Pledge of Allegiance, the Grisdale funeral, the Danny Pike affair—these things were noted, but they had no immediate impact on Stargirl's popularity at school. Not so with cheerleading and the boys' basketball season.

Chapter 11

▶ What did Stargirl do during the first quarter of each home game?

During the first quarter of each home game, Stargirl went over to the visitors' section and gave them a cheer. She began with an exaggerated ball-bouncing motion:

Dribble, Dribble!
Sis Boom Bibble!
We don't bite!
We don't nibble!
We just say—
(sweeping wave)
"Howwww-dee, friends!"
(two thumbs pointing to her chest)
"We're the Electrons!"
(points to them)
"Who—are—YYYYYOU?"
(turns head to side, cups ear)

A couple of visiting cheerleaders, maybe a fan or two would call back: "Wildcats!" or "Cougars!" or whatever, but most of them just gaped at her as if to say, Who is *this?* Some of her fellow cheerleaders were amused, some were <u>mortified</u>.

At that point the only crime Stargirl could have been accused of would be corniness. But she didn't stop there. She cheered whenever the ball went in the basket, regardless of which team shot it. It was the strangest sight: the other team scores, the MAHS crowd sits glumly on their hands while Stargirl, alone, pops up cheering.

▶ How did the other cheerleaders first try to control Stargirl?

At first the other cheerleaders tried to <u>suppress</u> her; it was like trying to calm down a puppy. When they gave her the pleated skirt, they made a cheerleader they never imagined. She did not limit herself to basketball games. She cheered anyone, anything, anytime. She cheered the big things—honors, election winners—but she gave most of her attention to little things.

---

words for everyday use

mor • ti • fied (môrt' ə fīd) *adj.,* shamed, humiliated. *I felt <u>mortified</u> when I found out I had failed my presentation.*

sup • press (sə pres') *v.,* inhibit; put down by force. *When the dancer was told to keep her movements more consistent with those around her, she felt <u>suppressed</u>.*

You never knew when it would happen. Maybe you were a little ninth-grade nobody named Eddie. As you're walking down the hall you see a candy wrapper on the floor. You pick it up and throw it in the nearest trash can—and suddenly there she is in front of you, pumping her arms, her honey hair and freckles flying, swallowing you whole with those enormous eyes, belting out a cheer she's making up on the spot, something about Eddie, Eddie and the trash can teaming up to wipe out litter. A mob is gathering, clapping hands in rhythm, more eyes on you than all the previous days of your life combined. You feel foolish, exposed, stupid. You want to follow the candy wrapper into the trash can. It's the most painful thing that's ever happened to you. Your brain keeps squirting out a single thought: *I'm going to die . . . I'm going to die . . .*

And so, when she finally finishes and her freckles settle back onto the bridge of her nose, why don't you? Why don't you just die?

Because they're clapping for you, that's why, and whoever heard of dying while they're clapping for you? And they're smiling at you. People who never even *saw* you before are smiling at you and slapping your back and pumping your hand, and suddenly it seems like the whole world is calling your name, and you're feeling so good you pretty much just float on home from school. And when you go to bed that night, the last thing you see before you zonk out are those eyes, and the last thing on your face is a smile.

Or maybe you showed up at school with really unusual earrings. Or you aced a test. Or broke your arm. Or got your braces off. Or maybe you weren't even a person. Maybe you were a charcoal drawing on the wall done by an art whiz. Or a really neat-looking bug out by the bike rack.

We wagged our heads and agreed what a goof girl this was, maybe even officially crazy, but we walked away smiling and maybe not saying but thinking the same thing: it felt good to get credit.

And if this had been any other year, things might have just gone on and on like that. But this was the year something unbelievable was happening on

▶ What was different about this year of basketball?

the basketball court. This was the year the team was winning. *Only* winning.

And that changed everything.

Early in the season no one noticed. Except for girls' tennis, we had never had good teams in anything. We expected to lose. We were comfortable with losing. In fact, most of us were <u>oblivious</u> to it, since we didn't even attend the games.

The year before, the basketball Electrons had won only five of twenty-six games. This year, they won their fifth game before Christmas. By early January they had won the tenth, and people began to notice that there was still a zero in the loss column.

"UNDEFEATED!" blared a sign on the plywood roadrunner. Some said we were winning by accident. Some said the other teams were simply more rotten than we were. Some thought the sign was a joke. One thing was certain: attendance went up. By the start of February the winning streak had reached sixteen, and there wasn't an empty seat in the gym.

But something even more interesting was happening. Suddenly we were no longer comfortable with losing. In fact, we forgot how to lose. The transformation was stunning in its speed. There was no apprenticeship period, no learning curve. No one had to teach us how to be winners. One day we were bored, indifferent, satisfied losers; the next we were <u>rabid</u> <u>fanatics</u>, stomping in the grandstand, painting our faces green and white, doing the wave as if we had been perfecting it for years.

We fell in love with our team. When we spoke of it, we used the word "we" instead of "they." The leading scorer, Brent Ardsley, seemed to have a golden glow about him as he moved through the school. And the more we loved our team, the more we hated

▶ What happened to the MAHS students the more they loved their team?

---

words for everyday use

obliv • i • ous (ə blĭ' vē əs) *adj.*, unaware; lacking attention. *I was <u>oblivious</u> to my mother calling me; I was concentrating on the show.*

rab • id (ra' bəd) *adj.*, going to extreme lengths in expressing a feeling, interest, or opinion. *After hearing the verdict, he had a <u>rabid</u> desire to throw his chair across the room.*

fa • na • tic (fə nat' ik) *n.*, person who holds extreme and unreasonable views; zealot. *My mother was a <u>fanatic</u> about a clean house—she was never satisfied.*

the opposition. We used to <u>envy</u> them. We even applauded them to spite our own <u>hapless</u> teams. Now we detested the opposition and everything about them. We hated their uniforms. We hated their coaches and their fans. We hated them because they were trying to spoil our perfect season. We resented every point scored against us. And how dare they celebrate!

We began to boo. It was our first experience as booers, but you'd have thought we were veterans. We booed the other team, we booed the other coach, we booed the other fans, the referees—whatever threatened our perfect season, we booed it.

We even booed the scoreboard. We hated games that went down to the wire. We hated suspense. We loved games that were decided in the first five minutes. We wanted more than victories, we wanted <u>massacres</u>. The only score we would have been totally happy with would have been 100 to 0.

And right there in the middle of it all, in the midst of this perfect season mania, was Stargirl, popping up whenever the ball went through the net, no matter which team scored, cheering everything and everybody. It was sometime in January when calls started flying from the stands: "Siddown." Then came the boos. She didn't seem to notice.

She did not seem to notice.

◄ How did Stargirl react to people booing her?

Of all the unusual features of Stargirl, this struck me as the most remarkable. Bad things did not stick to her. Correction: *her* bad things did not stick to her. *Our* bad things stuck very much to her. If we were hurt, if we were unhappy or otherwise <u>victimized</u> by life, she seemed to know about it and to care, as soon as we did. But bad things falling on her—unkind words, nasty stares, foot blisters—she seemed

---

words for everyday use

en • vy (en' vē) v., feel resentful awareness of an advantage enjoyed by another joined with a desire to possess the same advantage. *Patsy hated her brown, straight hair; she <u>envied</u> Georgina's blond, curly hair.*

hap • less (ha' pləs) adj., unfortunate. *My <u>hapless</u> attempt at playing football ended in a broken leg.*

mas • sa • cre (ma' si kər) n., act of complete destruction. *Our team's <u>massacre</u> over our biggest rivals came as a huge surprise.*

vic • tim • ize (vik' tə mīz') v., subject to deception or fraud. *When I discovered someone had forged my name on the petition, I felt <u>victimized</u>.*

unaware of. I never saw her look in a mirror, never heard her complain. All of her feelings, all of her attentions flowed outward. She had no ego.

The nineteenth game of the basketball season was played at Red Rock. In previous years cheerleaders had outnumbered Mica fans at away games. Not now. The <u>convoy</u> rolling across the desert that evening stretched for a couple of miles. By the time we were seated, there was barely room for the home-team fans.

It was the worst slaughter of the year. Red Rock was helpless. By the start of the fourth quarter we were ahead, 78 to 29. The coach put in the subs. We booed. We smelled a hundred points. We wanted blood. The coach put the starters back in. As we howled and thundered in the stands, Stargirl got up and walked from the gym. Those of us who noticed assumed she was going to the rest room. I kept glancing toward the exit. She never returned. With five seconds left in the game, the Electrons scored the hundredth point. We went nuts.

Stargirl had been outside the whole time, chatting with the bus driver. The other cheerleaders asked her why she left. She said she felt sorry for the Red Rock players. She felt her cheering was only making the massacre worse. Such games were no fun, she said. Your job isn't to have fun, they told her, your job is to cheer for Mica High no matter what. She just stared at them.

The team and the cheerleaders rode the same bus. When the players came out from the locker room, the cheerleaders told them what had happened. They devised a trick. They told Stargirl that someone had forgotten something in the gym, and would she please go get it. With Stargirl gone, they told the bus driver everyone was aboard, and the bus made the two-hour return trip without her.

▶ What do the cheerleaders tell Stargirl her job is as a cheerleader?

words for everyday use

con • voy (kän' vòi) *n.*, protective escort. *The <u>convoy</u> of children parading after the juggler proved his popularity.*

A Red Rock custodian drove her home that night. Next day in school, the cheerleaders told her it was all a big misunderstanding and acted as if they were sorry. She believed them.

The next day was February thirteenth. The Hot Seat.

Chapter 12

This is how *Hot Seat* went.

It took place in the communications center studio. There were two chairs on stage: the infamous Hot Seat itself—painted red with flames running up the legs—and an ordinary chair for the host, Kevin. Off to the side were two rows of six chairs each, the second row higher than the first. This was where the jury sat.

It was a jury in name only. The twelve members did not vote or <u>render</u> a verdict. Their job was to ask questions, to give the Hot Seat its heat: ticklish questions, embarrassing questions, nosy questions. But not mean or hurtful questions. The idea was to make the subject squirm, not roast.

In the spirit of mock <u>inquisition</u>, we called the subject the "victim." And why would anyone want to be the victim? The lure of TV. The chance to confess—or lie—before a camera and before peers instead of parents. But I doubted the usual reasons applied to Stargirl.

There were three cameras: one for the stage, one for the jury, and Chico. Chico was the handheld close-up camera. According to Mr. Robineau, our faculty advisor, a student named Chico once begged him to be a close-up camera kid. Mr. Robineau gave him a tryout, but Chico was so skinny he practically collapsed under the camera. The job went to someone else and Chico went to the weight room. By the following year Chico had muscles, and the camera was like nothing on his shoulder. He got the job, and he was brilliant at it. He gave the camera his own name. "We are one," he said. When he graduated, his name stayed behind, and from then on the close-up camera and its operator were a unit called Chico.

The host and the victim were each fitted with a thimble-size clip-on mike; the jury passed around a hand mike. Opposite the stage was the glassed-in

▶ *Why would anyone want to be the victim on* Hot Seat?

▶ *Where does Leo work?*

words for everyday use

ren • der (ren' dər) *v.,* present or submit. *He finally had to <u>render</u> an answer concerning the job offer.*

in • qui • si • tion (in' qwə zish' ən) *n.,* severe or intensive questioning. *My coach gave me a long <u>inquisition</u>, hoping to find out why I had missed three practices.*

control room, sound-insulated from the rest of the studio. That's where I worked, wearing my headset, watching the monitors, directing the shots. I stood at the shoulder of the technical director, or TD. He sat at a rack of buttons, punching up the shots I ordered. Also in the control room were the graphics and audio people. Mr. Robineau was there as faculty overseer, but basically the students worked everything.

Kevin's job was to get things started: intro the victim, ask a few opening questions, stir things up if the jury was slow. Usually the jury was on the ball. Typical questions: "Does it bother you that you're so short?" Is it true that you like so-and-so?" "Do you wish you were good-looking?" "How often do you take a shower?"

It almost always added up to entertainment. At the end of the half hour, as we cued credits and music, there was always a good feeling in the air, and every-one—victim, jury members, studio crew—mingled and became students again.

We filmed the shows after school, then broadcast them that night—prime time—on local cable. About ten thousand homes. Our own surveys said at least fifty percent of the student body watched any given show. We outdrew most of the hot sitcoms. We expected to top ninety percent for the Stargirl show.

◀ When and where does the public see Hot Seat?

But I had a secret: I wished no one would watch.

In the month since we had scheduled the show, Stargirl's popularity had dropped out of sight. Gone were ukuleles from the lunchroom. More and more kids saw her cheerleading behavior as <u>undermining</u> the basketball team and its perfect record. I was afraid the boos for her might spread from the court to the studio. I was afraid the show might turn ugly.

When Stargirl came in that day after school, Kevin gave her the usual briefing while Mr. Robineau and I checked out the equipment. As the jury members

words for everyday use	un • der • mine (ən dər mīn') v., weaken or ruin. I didn't want to <u>undermine</u> Bill's decision, so I remained quiet.

straggled in, they were not clowning around or tap-dancing on the stage as jurors usually did. They went right to their seats. Stargirl was the one tap-dancing. And mugging for the cameras with Cinnamon the rat licking her nose. Kevin was cracking up, but the faces of the jurors were grim. One of them was Hillari Kimble. My bad feeling got worse.

I retreated to the control room and shut the door. I checked communications with the cameras. We were ready. Kevin and Stargirl took their seats. I took one last look through the plate glass that separated the set from the control room. For the next half hour I would see the world through four monitors. "Okay, everybody," I announced, "here we go." I cut the studio mike. I looked over my controlroom mates. "We all set?" Everyone nodded.

Just then Stargirl lifted one of Cinnamon's front paws and waved it at the control room and said in a squeaky voice, "Hi, Leo."

I froze. I came <u>unraveled</u>. I didn't know she knew my name. I just stood there like a dummy. Finally I waggled my fingers at the rat and mouthed the words "Hi, Cinnamon," although they couldn't hear me on the other side of the glass.

I took a deep breath. "Okay, ready music, ready intro." I paused. "Music, intro."

▶ What moment does Leo live for?

This was the moment I lived for, launching the show. I was the director, the maestro, I called the shots. On the monitors before me I watched the program unfold according to my commands. But on this day the thrill was missing. I felt only a dark dread snaking along the cables.

"Greetings . . . and welcome to *Hot Seat* . . ."

Kevin went through the opening spiel.[1] Kevin loved to be on camera. He was ideal for a show like

---

1. **opening spiel.** Opening speech

---

words for everyday use

un • rav • el (ən raʹ vəl) v., come apart. *Once the new evidence came into play, Kate's theory began to <u>unravel</u>.*

this, which made good use of his smirky grin and arching, Did-I-really-hear-you-say-that? eyebrows.

He turned to Stargirl. Then, <u>impromptu</u>, he reached out and stroked the nose of Cinnamon, who was perched on Stargirl's shoulder. "Want to hold him?" she said.

Kevin gave the camera a Should-I look. "Sure," he said.

"Ready, Chico, rat," I said into my headset mike.

"Ready" was always first in the command sequence.

Chico zoomed in.

"Chico."

TD punched up Chico. The camera followed Cinnamon from Stargirl's hands to Kevin's. No sooner was the rat in Kevin's lap than it scampered up his chest and darted between two buttons into his shirt. Kevin yipped and squirmed. "It scratches!"

◄ What did the rat do once it landed in Kevin's lap?

"He has fingernails," Stargirl said calmly. "He won't hurt you."

Chico nailed Cinnamon poking his head out from between the two buttons. Mr. Robineau stuck a thumbs-up in front of my face.

Kevin gave the camera his Ain't-I-something face. He turned again to Stargirl. "You know, ever since you showed up at school this year, we've been wanting to put you on the Hot Seat."

Stargirl stared at him. She turned to the live camera. Her eyes were growing wider . . .

Something was happening.

. . . and wider . . .

"Chico!" I barked.

Chico moved in, crouching, giving it a little upshot. Terrific. "Closer, closer," I said.

Stargirl's wonderstruck eyes practically filled the screen. I checked the long-shot monitor. She was frozen, rigid, as if electrified to the chair.

---

words for everyday use im • promp • tu (im präm′ tü) *adj.*, without preparation or advance thought. *Shirley gave an impromptu guitar performance after Jake mentioned his love of guitar music.*

► What does Mr. Robineau notice about how Stargirl is taking Hot Seat?

Someone smacked my shoulder. I turned. Mr. Robineau was laughing, saying something. I lifted one earphone. "She's *joking*," he repeated. And suddenly I saw. She was taking "Hot Seat" literally. She was milking it for all it was worth, and judging from the blank stares of Kevin and the jury, Mr. Robineau and I were the only ones who got the joke.

Stargirl's hands were rising now from the arms of the Hot Seat . . .

"Ready one," I called. "One!"

Camera One, not there at first but getting it now, the long shot, nailing her as her hands came off the chair arms, fingers spread wide, you could almost see her fingertips smoking . . .

Hold it, I prayed, *hold it . . .*

. . . as her horrified eyes swung down over the side of the chair, the Hot Seat, saw the painted flames . . .

"EEEEEEEEEEEYIKES!"

Her scream bent instrument dials like palms in a hurricane. The rat leaped from Kevin's shirt. The TV image quaked as my Camera One man flinched, but he recovered and caught her standing now on the front edge of the stage, bending over with her rear end in the camera, flapping her hands behind her, fanning her smoking fanny.

Finally Kevin got it. He went nuts.

"One pull back, get Kevin in it. Ready . . . One."

Kevin was doubled up, tipping out of his chair, on his knees on the stage. His laughter flooded the control room. The rat ran over his hands and hopped down the single stage step . . .

"The rat!" I yelled. "Two, get the rat!"

But Two couldn't get the rat because the rat was nosing around Two's feet and Two was bolting from his camera.

"Chico, rat!"

► How did Chico get the shot of the rat heading to the jury?

Chico dived. He was flat on the floor, feeding the live screen a brilliant shot of the rat heading over to the jury, the jury members scrambling, taking off, climbing onto their seats.

Forget the "Readys"; things were happening too fast. The cameras were dancing, feeding the monitors. I barked commands. TD was punching his button rack like some hard-rock keyboarder.

Stargirl's <u>pantomime</u> remains the best I have ever seen. Mr. Robineau kept squeezing my shoulder. As he said later, it was the greatest moment in *Hot Seat* history.

But because of what followed, no audience would ever see it.

words for everyday use
pan • to • mime (pan' tə mīm) *n.*, dramatic presentation given without words, using only action and gestures. *Through an elaborate <u>pantomime</u>, he was able to show us what happened without using any words.*

Chapter 13

In less than a minute, everything returned to normal. Stargirl retrieved Cinnamon and sat back coolly in the Hot Seat as if nothing had happened. Kevin's eyes twinkled. He was squirming. He couldn't wait to dig into the interview. Neither could the jury, but their eyes were not twinkling.

Kevin forced himself to look serious. "So, your name. Stargirl. It's pretty unusual."

Stargirl gave him a blank look.

Kevin was flustered. "Isn't it?" he said.

Stargirl shrugged. "Not to me."

She's putting him on, I thought. "Chico," I said into my mike, "stay tight on her face."

A voice was heard dimly off-camera. Kevin turned. A jury member had spoken. "Jury mike up," I said. "Ready Two." The mike was passed to Jennifer St. John. "Two."

The mike looked like a black ice cream cone before Jennifer's face. Her voice wasn't pleasant. "What was wrong with the name your parents gave you?"

Stargirl turned slowly to Jennifer. She smiled. "Nothing. It was a good name."

"What was it?"

"Susan."

"So why did you drop it?"

"Because I didn't feel like Susan anymore."

"So you just threw out Susan and named yourself Stargirl."

"No." Still smiling.

"No?"

"Pocket Mouse."

Twelve pairs of eyes boggled.

"What?"

"I named myself Pocket Mouse," Stargirl said breezily. "Then Mudpie. Then Hullygully. *Then* Stargirl."

Damon Ricci snatched the mike from Jennifer St. John. "So what's it gonna be next? Dog Turd?"

Uh-oh, I thought, *here we go.*

Kevin jumped in. "So . . . you change your name whenever you get tired of it?"

▶ What was Stargirl's birth name?

"Whenever it doesn't fit anymore. I'm not my name. My name is something I wear, like a shirt. It gets worn, I outgrow it, I change it."

"So why Stargirl?"

"Oh, I don't know." She petted Cinnamon's nose with her fingertip. "I was walking in the desert one night, looking up at the sky—like," she chuckled, "how can you *not* look at the sky!—and it just sort of came to me, fell onto me."

Kevin looked up from his sheet of prepared questions. "So what do your parents think? Are they sad you didn't keep Susan?"

"No. It was almost their idea. When I started calling myself Pocket Mouse when I was little, they called me that, too. And we just never went back."

Another distant voice from the jury.

I tapped the soundman. "Jury mike. And keep all mikes open." I hated to do it.

◀ What does Leo do that he hates doing?

It was Mike Ebersole. "I said, do you love your country?"

"Yes," she answered briskly. "Do you love yours?"

Ebersole ignored her question. "Why don't you say the Pledge of Allegiance right?"

She smiled. "Sounds right to me."

"Sounds like you're a traitor to me."

Jurors were only supposed to ask questions, not make statements.

A hand reached into the picture and grabbed the mike from Ebersole. Becca Rinaldi's angry face appeared on Camera Two. "Why do you cheer for the other team?"

Stargirl seemed to be thinking it over. "I guess because I'm a cheerleader."

◀ What is Stargirl's reason for cheering the other team?

"You're not *just* a cheerleader, you dumb cluck"— Becca Rinaldi was snarling into the mike—"you're supposed to be *our* cheerleader. A *Mica* cheerleader."

I glanced at Mr. Robineau. He was turned away from the monitors. He was staring straight at the set through the control room window.

Stargirl was leaning forward, looking earnestly at Becca Rinaldi, her voice small as a little girl's. "When the other team scores a point and you see how happy it makes all their fans, doesn't it make you happy, too?"

Becca growled, "No."

"Doesn't it make you want to join in?"

"No."

"Don't you ever want the other team to be happy, too?"

"No."

Stargirl seemed genuinely surprised. "You don't always want to be the winner . . . do you?"

Becca scowled at her, jutted out her jaw. "Yes. Yes, I do. Yes. I *always* want to be the winner. That's what I do. I root for us to win. That's what we all do." She swept her arm around the set. "We root for Mica." She jabbed her finger at the stage. "Who do you root for?"

▶ *Who does Stargirl root for?*

Stargirl hesitated. She smiled, she threw out her arms. "I root for *everybody!*"

Kevin—to the rescue, thankfully—clapped his hands. "Hey—how about this? Maybe it should be official. Maybe one person in the whole district should be appointed to be on"—he waved his arm—"everybody's side!"

Stargirl reached over and slapped Kevin's knee. "She could wear every school's letter on her sweater!"

Kevin laughed. "She'd have to be big as a house!"

Stargirl slapped her own knee. "Then no letter at all. That's even better." She looked into the camera, she swiped at the space before her. "Out with letters!"

"Cheerleader-at-large!"

"Everybody's cheerleader!"

Kevin sat at attention, placed his hand over his heart. "With liberty and justice . . . and a cheerleader for all."

Ebersole snarled into the jury mike: "And a nut roll for all."

Kevin wagged his finger. "That's a no-no," he scolded. "No statements from the jury. Questions only."

Renee Bozeman snatched the mike. "Okay, here's a question. Why did you quit homeschooling?"

Stargirl's face became serious. "I wanted to make friends."

"Well, you sure have a funny way of showing it, making the whole school mad at you."

I wished I had never given in to Hot-Seating Stargirl.

Stargirl just stared. Chico filled the screen with her face.

"Gimme—" It was Jennifer St. John, reaching for the mike. "And out of school, too. You <u>meddle</u> into everybody's business. You stick your nose in, whether you're invited or not. Why do you do that?"

Stargirl had no reply. Her usual <u>impish</u> expression was gone. She looked at Jennifer. She looked at the camera, as if trying to find an answer in the lens. Then she was looking away, looking at the control room. I took my eyes from the monitor and for a second I thought they met hers at the control room window.

◄ How does Stargirl look at the camera?

I had been wondering when Hillari Kimble would speak up. Now she did. "I'm gonna tell you something, girl. You're goofy. You're crazy." Hillari was standing, jabbing her finger at Stargirl, chewing on the mike. "You must've come from *Mars* or something . . ." Kevin raised a timid hand. "And don't you tell me 'no statements,' Kevin. Where'd you come from, Mars or something? There, now it's a question. Why don't you go back to where you came from? There's another question."

Stargirl's eyes filled the camera. *Don't cry,* I prayed.

There was no stopping Hillari. "You want to cheer for other schools? Fine! Go there! Don't come to *my* school. Get outta *my* school!"

Other hands were snatching at the mike.

"I know what your problem is. All this weird stuff you do? It's just to get attention."

"It's to get a boyfriend!"

The jurors laughed. They were a mob. Hands grabbed at the mike. Kevin looked anxiously at me. I could do nothing. With all the buttons and switches

| words for everyday use | med • dle (med′ əl) v., interfere in something that is not one's business. *She did not want to meddle in his affairs—he needed to work out his own problems.* | imp • ish (im′ pish) *adj.,* mischievous. *His impish ways resulted in an afternoon in detention.* |

at my command, I was helpless to change anything on the other side of the glass.

"I got a simple question for you. What's the matter with you? Huh? *Huh?"*

"Why can't you be normal?"

"Why do you wanna be so different?"

"Yeah—is something wrong with us, you gotta be so different?"

"Why don't you wear makeup?"

They were all standing now, jabbing, jutting, shouting, whether they had the mike or not.

"You don't like us, do you? *Do* you?"

Mr. Robineau flipped the master toggle on the console.[1] "That's it," he said.

I flipped the studio sound switch. "That's it. Show's over."

The jury went on shouting.

---

1. **flipped the master toggle on the console**. Turned off the master switch of the device that allows an operator to monitor and interact with a system

Respond to the Selection

Imagine that you had been on the jury of *Hot Seat*. What questions would you have asked Stargirl? Based on how she responded to other questions on *Hot Seat*, how do you think she would have answered your questions?

Investigate, Inquire, and Imagine

Recall: Gathering Facts

1a. What did Stargirl do while the other cheerleaders were taking breaks during the football games? Where did she go?

2a. After the "Undefeated!" sign describing the basketball team goes up on the roadrunner, what happens to the MAHS students' views of losing?

3a. When Renee asks Stargirl why she quit homeschooling, what is Stargirl's response?

Interpret: Finding Meaning

→ 1b. Why do you think she did this?

→ 2b. What insight does this give you to how people respond to winning? What are the pros and cons to this response?

→ 3b. Do you think Stargirl has made good choices in trying to achieve her goal? Why, or why not?

Analyze: Taking Things Apart

4a. The students of MAHS change their feelings toward Stargirl from liking her to disliking her. Find examples of things Stargirl does that contribute to this change.

Synthesize: Bringing Things Together

→ 4b. What effect do you think the students' dislike toward Stargirl will have on Stargirl? on the student body as a whole? to the basketball season?

Evaluate: Making Judgments

5a. Leo describes Stargirl as having no ego—that she thinks only of others and not herself. He says that she seems oblivious to bad things directed toward her, but cares deeply about bad things that happen to other people. Do you agree or disagree with his assessment?

Extend: Connecting Ideas

→ 5b. Is having an ego necessary? Is an ego a negative thing or a positive thing? Explain your answer.

Understanding Literature

Conflict. A **conflict** is a struggle between two people or things in a literary work. Describe the conflict between Stargirl and the students at MAHS.

Mood. **Mood,** or atmosphere is the emotion created in the reader by a piece of writing. A writer creates a mood through the use of concrete details. Examine the scene in chapter 12, when Stargirl pretends to be sitting on a hot seat—literally. Identify six concrete details used by Spinelli and the mood these details create.

Dialogue. **Dialogue** is conversation involving two or more people or characters. Examine the dialogue between the jurors and Stargirl in chapter 13. How does this conversation make Leo feel? What do you think is the significance of this dialogue?

Chapter 14

This was the start of a period that blurs as I try to recall it. Incidents seem to <u>cascade</u> and merge. Events become feelings, feelings become events. Head and heart are contrary historians.

The *Hot Seat* session was never aired. Mr. Robineau destroyed the tape. Of course, that didn't stop every moment of it from being reported. In fact, most of the students knew about it by the time school opened next day.

◀ What does Mr. Robineau do with the tape?

What I recall then, when the last detail had been spilled, is a period of whispers and waiting. Tension. What would happen now? Would the jury's open hostility spill over into the classrooms? How would Stargirl react? Answers were expected on the following day, Valentine's Day. On previous holidays— Halloween, Thanksgiving, Christmas, Groundhog Day—Stargirl had left a little something on each desk in her homeroom. Would she do likewise this time?

The answer was yes. Each member of Homeroom 17 found a candy heart on his or her desk that morning.

There was a basketball game that night; that I do remember. The biggest game of the year. The Electrons had breezed through the regular season undefeated, but now the second season was about to begin: the play-offs. First the districts, then the regionals, and finally the state tournament. We had never even made it to the districts, but now visions of championships danced in our heads. The Electrons—champions of all Arizona! We would settle for nothing less.

First hurdle in our way was Sun Valley, champions of the Pima League. The game was played Valentine's night on a neutral court in Casa Grande. All of Mica, it seemed, emptied out and headed for the game. Kevin and I went in the pickup.

---

words for everyday use

cas • cade (kas kād') v., fall. *The events of the day began to <u>cascade</u> until I was unclear about exactly what happened.*

▶ How does Leo feel when Stargirl begins cheering only for MAHS?

From the moment the Mica mob entered the gym, our cheers rattled the rafters. The big green *M* on Stargirl's white sweater flounced as she spun and leaped with the other cheerleaders. I spent as much time watching her as I did watching the game. She cheered when we scored. When Sun Valley scored, she did not. Something inside me felt better.

But not for long. We were losing. For the first time all year, we were trailing at the end of the first quarter. In fact, we were getting smoked, 21 to 9. The reason was no mystery. While Sun Valley's team was not as good as ours, they did have one thing we did not: a superstar. A kid named Ron Kovac. He stood six-foot-eight and averaged thirty points per game. Our players looked like five Davids flailing against Goliath.

Sun Valley's lead had increased to nineteen points midway through the second quarter. Our once-raucous fans were stunned into silence, and that's when it happened. The ball was loose in the middle of the floor. Several players from each team dived for it. At that moment Kovac was running past, trying to avoid the divers, and his right foot came down on a prone player's sneaker—so it was told in the newspapers the next day. At the time, it happened so fast no one saw it, though several people said they heard a sickening crack, like a twig snapping. All we knew was that suddenly Goliath was on the floor writhing and screaming, and his right foot looked all wrong, and the Sun Valley coaches and trainer and players were sprinting across the floor. But they were not the first. Stargirl, somehow, was already there.

▶ Who gets to Kovac first?

While Kovac's own cheerleaders sat gaping and stricken on their bench, Stargirl knelt on the hardwood floor. She held his head in her lap while the others attended his broken leg. Her hands moved over his face and forehead. She seemed to be saying things to him. When they carried him away on a stretcher, she followed. Everyone—both sides—stood

words for everyday use

rau • cous (rô′ kəs) *adj.*, loud and disorderly. The _raucous_ teenagers at the mall were asked to leave unless they quieted down immediately.

writhe (rīth′) *v.*, twist or turn. *When Danielle broke her ankle, she fell to the floor, writhing in pain.*

and applauded. The Sun Valley cheerleaders leaped as if he had just scored two points. Ambulance lights flashed in the high windows.

I knew why I was applauding, but I wondered about some of the other Mica fans. Were they really standing in tribute, or because they were happy to see him go?

The game resumed. Stargirl returned to the cheerleaders' bench. Without Kovac, Sun Valley was a pushover. By early in the second half we took the lead and went on to win easily.

Two nights later we lost to Glendale. Again we fell farther and farther behind as the first half went on. But this time there was no turnaround in the second half. This time the Electrons faced not one but five players better than themselves. This time no opponent broke an ankle, though I'm sure in our desperation some of us secretly wished for it.

We were shocked. We couldn't believe it. And then, as the seconds of the fourth quarter ticked by, we did believe. The cheers from across the gym were like volleys of arrows piercing our grand <u>delusion</u>. How could we have been so stupid? Did we really think that little Mica, undefeated in its own third-rate league, could ever stand up to the big-city powerhouses around the state? We had been lured into great, foolish expectations. Suckered. We were devastated. It had been so wonderful to be winners. And so right for us. Winning, we had come to believe, was our destiny.

And now . . .

As the Glendale coach sent in the scrubs to mop us up, Mica girls wept. Boys cursed and booed. Some blamed the officials. Or the nets. Or the lights. The cheerleaders, to their credit, kept on cheering. They looked up at us with glistening eyes and mascara tracks on their cheeks. They pumped their arms and shouted and did everything that cheerleaders are

◀ *What had the students of MAHS come to believe about winning?*

---

words for everyday use   de • lu • sion (di loo′ zhən) *n.*, incorrect perception of reality. *He was under the <u>delusion</u> that I liked him; I did not.*

supposed to do, but their gestures were empty, their hearts not in it.

Except for Stargirl. As I watched her intently, I could see that she was different. Her cheeks were dry. There was no crack in her voice, no sag in her shoulders. From the start of the second half on, she never sat down. And she never again looked at the game. She turned her back on the court. She stood and faced us and gave not an ounce of herself to the <u>jubilation</u> across the gym. We were losing by thirty points with a minute to go, but she cheered on as if we had a chance. Her eyes blazed with a ferocity I had never seen before. She shook her fists at us. She flung her <u>defiance</u> at our gloom.

And then her face was bloody.

A Glendale player had just dunked the ball and Kevin pounded my knee with his fist and I looked to see Stargirl's face suddenly a bloody mask and I was on my feet screaming, "NOOOOO!"

But it wasn't blood. It was a tomato. Someone had splattered her face with a perfectly thrown ripe tomato, and as the clock expired and the Glendale fans poured onto the court, Stargirl just stood there, her great eyes staring up at us in utter bewilderment through the pulpy red gore. Spouts of bitter laughter erupted among us, even some applause.

The next morning at home I found the card. It was in a school notebook that apparently I had not opened for several days. It was a valentine, one of those little cut-out third-grade sorts, showing a blushing little boy and a girl with mary jane shoes and a big red heart between them and the words "I LOVE YOU." And as third-graders—and high-schoolers—often do, the sender had signed it in code:

▶ What did a student throw at Stargirl?

words for everyday use

ju • bi • la • tion (jōō′ bə lā′ shən) *n.,* rejoicing. *When her candidate was announced the winner, Sheila was filled with jubilation.*

de • fi • ance (də fī′ əns) *n.,* open disregard for authority or opposition. *In defiance of the non-smoking sign, the young rebel lit a cigarette.*

Chapter 15

She gave everybody in school a card. That was my first thought.

When I saw Kevin at school, I was about to ask him, but I pulled back. I waited until lunch. I tried to be casual. I slipped it in with the only thing that mattered that day. The school was in mourning. The game. The loss. The tomato. Oh yeah, <u>incidentally</u>, speaking of Stargirl: "Did you happen to get a card?"

He looked at me funny. "She gave them to her homeroom, I heard."

"Yeah," I said, "that's what I heard, too. But was that all? Didn't she give them to everybody else?"

He shrugged. "Not to me. Why? You get one?"

◀ What does Kevin not get from Stargirl?

He was looking away across the lunchroom, biting into his sandwich, yet I felt he was grilling me. I shook my head. "Oh no, just wondering."

Actually, I was sitting on the card. It was in the back pocket of my jeans. Meanwhile, all eyes in the lunchroom were on Stargirl. I think we half expected to see traces of red still clinging to her face. She sat at her usual table with Dori Dilson and several other friends. She seemed <u>subdued</u>. She did not play her ukulele. She did not play with her rat. She just ate and talked with the girls at her table.

As the lunch period was ending, she got up but did not head straight for the exit. Instead she detoured in the direction of my table. I panicked. I jumped up, grabbed my stuff, blurted "Gotta go," left Kevin with his mouth hanging, and took off. Not fast enough. Halfway to the door I heard her behind me: "Hi, Leo." My face got warm. I was sure every eye was turned to me. I was sure they could all see the card in my pocket. I pretended to look at the clock. I pretended I was late for something. I ran from the lunchroom.

◀ How does Leo avoid Stargirl in the lunchroom?

I lurked in the shadows for the rest of the day. I went straight home after school. I stayed in my

---

words for everyday use

in • ci • den • tal • ly (in sə den' təl ē) *adv.,* by way of interjection, by the way. *Incidentally, Sharon won't return until noon.*

sub • dued (sub dood') *adj.,* controlled or repressed emotionally. *Her <u>subdued</u> mood worried me; I wanted her to open up and talk to me.*

room. I came out only for dinner. I told my parents I had a project to do. I paced. I lay on my bed and stared at the ceiling. I stared out the window. I laid the card on my study desk. I picked it up. I read it. I read it. I read it. I played "Hi, Leo" over and over in my head. I tossed darts at the corkboard on the back of my door. My father called in, "What's your project, darts?" I went out. I drove around in the pickup. I drove down her street. At the last intersection before her house, I turned off.

For hours I lay under my sheet of moonlight. Her voice came through the night, from the light, from the stars.

Hi, Leo.

In the morning—it was a Saturday—Kevin and I went together to Archie's for the weekly meeting of the Loyal Order of the Stone Bone. There were about fifteen of us. We wore our fossil necklaces. Archie wanted to discuss the Eocene skull he was holding, but all the others could talk about was the game. When they told Archie about the tomato, his eyebrows went up, but other than that, his face did not change. I thought, *This is not news to him, he already knows.*

Archie spent the whole session that way, nodding and smiling and raising his eyebrows. We dumped our disappointment on him, the devastation of the loss. He said very little. When it was over, he looked down at the skull in his lap and patted it and said, "Well, this fellow here lost his game, too. He was winning for ten million years or so, but then the early grasses started growing up around him, and he found himself in a different league. He hung in there as well as he could. He scored his points, but he kept falling farther and farther behind. The opposition was better, quicker, keener. In the championship game, our boy got <u>annihilated</u>. Not only didn't he

▶ *What does Archie want to discuss?*

---

words for everyday use

an • ni • hi • late (a nī' ə lāt') v., destroy completely. *After the children spent hours building their sand castle, they took great fun in <u>annihilating</u> it.*

show up for class the next day, he never showed up, period. They never saw him again."

Archie lifted the snouted, fox-size skull until it was side by side with his own face. A good minute passed as he said nothing, inviting us into our own thoughts. Faces staring at faces staring at faces. Tens of millions of years of faces in a living room in a place called Arizona.

Chapter 16

Monday. Lunch.

This time I stayed put when Stargirl came toward my table on her way out. My back was to her. I could see Kevin's eyes following her, widening as she came closer. And then his eyes stopped, and his mouth was sliding toward a wicked grin, and it seemed like everything stopped but the clink of pans in the kitchen, and the back of my neck was on fire.

"You're welcome," I heard her say, almost sing.

I thought, *What?* but then I knew what. And I knew what I had to do. I knew I had to turn around and speak to her, and I knew she was going to stand there until I did. This was silly, this was childish, this being terrified of her. What was I afraid of, anyway?

I turned. I felt heavy, as if I were moving through water, as if I were confronting much more than a tenth-grade girl with an unusual name. I faced the gaudy sunflower on her canvas bag—it looked hand-painted—and at last my eyes fell into hers. I said, "Thanks for the card."

Her smile put the sunflower to shame. She walked off.

Kevin was grinning, wagging his head. "She's in love."

▶ What does Kevin tell Leo after Stargirl leaves the lunch table?

"Bull," I said.

"She is mucho in love."

"She's goofy, that's all."

The bell rang. We gathered our stuff and left.

I wobbled through the rest of the day. A baseball bat could not have hit me harder than that smile did. I was sixteen years old. In that time, how many thousands of smiles had been aimed at me? So why did this one feel like the first?

After school my feet carried me toward her homeroom. I was trembling. My stomach had flies. I had no idea what I was going to do if I saw her. I only knew I couldn't *not* go.

She wasn't there. I hurried through the hallways. I ran outside. The buses were loading. Cars were revving. Hundreds of kids were scattering. For months she had been everywhere, now she was nowhere.

I heard her name. *Her name.* The same two syllables, the same eight letters that I had been hearing all year, and suddenly the sound struck my ear with a *ping* of pure silver. I drifted sideways to overhear. A group of girls was chattering toward a bus.

"When?"

"Today. After school. Just now!"

"I don't believe it!"

"I don't believe it took so long."

"Kicked off? Are they allowed?"

"Sure. Why not? It's not *her* school."

"I would've kicked her off long ago. It was <u>treason</u>."

"Good riddance."

I knew what they were talking about. It had been rumored for days. Stargirl had been kicked off the cheerleading squad.

◄ What happens to Stargirl's position as a cheerleader?

"Hi, Leo!"

A chorus of girl voices calling my name. I turned. They were in front of the sun. I shaded my eyes. They sang in unison: "Starboy!" They laughed. I waved and hurried home. I could never have admitted it, but I was thrilled.

Her house was two miles from mine, behind a little ten-store shopping center. Archie had told me where. I walked. I didn't want to ride. I wanted to be slow about it. I wanted to feel myself getting closer step by step, feel the tension rising like fizz in a soda bottle.

I did not know what I would do if I saw her. I knew only that I was nervous, afraid. I was more comfortable with her as history than as person. Suddenly, <u>intensely</u>, I wanted to know everything about her. I wanted to see her baby pictures. I wanted to watch her eating breakfast, wrapping a gift, sleeping. Since September she had been a performer—unique and outrageous—on the high school stage. She was the opposite of cool; she held nothing back. From her decorated desk to her

---

words for everyday use

treas • on (trē′ zən) *n.*, betrayal of a trust. *It felt like <u>treason</u> when I found out my best friend had stolen my bracelet.*

in • tense (in ten(t)s′) *adj.*, very strong, extreme. *Her <u>intense</u> desire to learn piano led her to become a dedicated musician.* **intensely,** *adv.*

oratorical speech to her performance on the football field, she was there for all to see. And yet now I felt I had not been paying attention. I felt I had missed something, something important.

She lived on Palo Verde. For a person so different, her house was surprisingly ordinary, at least by Arizona standards. Single story. Pale adobe.[1] Clay-red pipetile roof. Not a blade of grass in the small front yard, but rather barrel and prickly pear cacti and clusters of stones.

▶ What does Leo realize he might be mistaken for?

It was dark, as I had intended, when I got there. I walked up and down the other side of the street. It occurred to me I might be mistaken for a prowler, so I walked around the block. I stopped into Roma Delite for a slice of pizza. Gulped down only half of it, hurried back out, couldn't relax when her house was not in sight. Couldn't relax when it was.

At first it was enough just to see the house. Then I began to wonder if she was inside. I wondered what she could be doing. Light came from every window I could see. There was a car in the driveway. The longer I hung around, the closer I wanted to be. I crossed the street and practically dashed past the house. As I went by, I scooped up a stone from the yard. I went up the street, turned, and looked at her house in the distance.

I whispered to the salt-sprinkled sky, "That's where Stargirl Caraway lives. She likes me."

I headed back toward the house. The street, the sidewalks were deserted. The stone was warm in my hand. This time I walked slowly as I approached. I felt strange. My eyes fixed on a triangle of light in a curtained window. I saw a shadow on a yellow wall. I seemed to be drifting, footless, into the light.

▶ What does Leo do when the front door opens?

Suddenly the front door opened. I dived behind the car in the driveway and crouched by the rear fender. I heard the door close. I heard steps. The steps matched the movement of a long shadow cast down the driveway. My breath stopped. The shadow stopped. I felt both ridiculous and weirdly, perfectly placed, as if crouching by that car was precisely what life had in store for me at that moment.

---

1. **adobe.** Brick or building material of sun-dried earth and straw

Her voice came from beyond the shadow. "Remember when you followed me into the desert that day after school?"

Absurdly, I debated whether to answer, as if doing so would—what? Give me away? I leaned into the smooth metal of the fender. It never occurred to me to stand, to show myself. Hours seemed to pass before I finally croaked, "Yes."

"Why did you turn around and go back?"

Her tone was casual, as if she held conversations every night with people crouching behind the car in the driveway.

"I don't remember," I said.

"Were you afraid?"

"No," I lied.

"I wouldn't have let you get lost, you know."

"I know."

A little shadow detached itself from the larger one. It came toward me, wavering over the pebbled driveway. It had a tail. It wasn't a shadow. It was the rat, Cinnamon. Cinnamon stopped at the tip of one of my sneakers. He stood, looking up at me. He put his front paws on top of my sneaker and nosed into the laces.

◀ What comes to Leo and stops by his sneaker?

"Are you getting acquainted with Cinnamon?"

"Sort of."

"Are you lying?"

"Sort of."

"Are you afraid of rats?"

"Sort of."

"Do you think I'm cute? If you say sort of, I'll tell Cinnamon to bite you."

"Yes."

"Yes what?"

"I think you're cute." I thought of adding "sort of" just to be funny, but I didn't.

"Do you think Cinnamon is cute?"

The rat had climbed fully onto my sneaker now. I could feel his weight. I wanted to shake him off. His tail spilled onto the driveway. "No comment," I said.

"Oh my, hear that, Cinnamon? No comment. He doesn't want people to know he thinks you're cute."

"I think you're getting a little carried away," I said.

▶ What does Stargirl propose Leo do with Cinnamon?

"I certainly hope so," she said. "Nothing's more fun than being carried away. Would you like to carry Cinnamon away for the night? He loves sleep-overs."

"No thank you."

"Oh." Her voice was mock-pouty. "Are you sure? He's no trouble. He hardly takes up any room. All you have to feed him is a Mini Wheat. Or two grapes. And he won't poop on your rug. Will you, Cinnamon? Go ahead, stand up and tell him you won't. Stand up, Cinnamon."

Cinnamon stood on my sneaker. His eyes shone like black pearls.

"Doesn't he have the cutest ears?"

Who notices a rat's ears? I looked. She was right. "Yeah," I said, "I guess he does."

"Tickle him behind his ears. He loves that."

I swallowed hard. I reached down with the tips of my two forefingers and tickled the tiny, furry spaces behind the rat's ears. I guessed he enjoyed it. He didn't move. And then, surprising myself, I moved one fingertip in front of his nose, and he licked me. It had never occurred to me that rats do that. His tongue was half the size of my little fingernail. I would have guessed it was rough, like a cat's, but it wasn't; it was smooth.

▶ Where does Cinnamon go after sitting on Leo's foot?

And then he was no longer on my foot—he was on my shoulder. I yelped. I tried to swat him off, but he dug into my shirt with his fingernails. Meanwhile, Stargirl was cracking up. I could see the shadow shaking.

"Let me guess," she said. "Cinnamon jumped onto your shoulder."

"You got it," I said.

"And you're thinking about how rats are supposed to go for people's throats."

"I wasn't," I said, "but now that you mention it . . ." I clamped my hands around my neck. I felt something in my ear. Whiskery. I yelped again. "He's eating my ear!"

Stargirl laughed some more. "He's nuzzling you. He likes you. Especially your ears. He never meets an ear he doesn't love. By the time he's done, that ear of yours will be clean as a whistle. Especially if there's some leftover peanut butter in it."

I could feel the tiny tongue mopping the crevices of my left ear. "It tickles!" I felt something else. "I feel teeth!"

"He's just scraping something off for you. You must have something crusty in there. Have you washed your ears lately?"

"None of your business."

"Sorry. Didn't mean to get personal."

"I forgive you."

All was quiet for a while, except for the snuffing in my ear. I could hear the rat breathing. His tail drooped into my front shirt pocket.

"Do you want to confess now?"

"Confess what?" I said.

"That you're actually starting to like having a rodent poking around in your ear."

I smiled. I nodded, <u>dislodging</u> the rat's nose for a moment. "I confess."

More silence, tiny breathing in my ear.

"Well," she said at last, "we have to go in now. Say good night, Cinnamon."

No, I thought, *don't go.*

"I still have another ear," I said.

"If he does that one, he'll never want to leave you, and I'll be jealous. Come on, Cinnamon. Time for beddy bye."

Cinnamon went on snuffing.

"He's not coming, is he?"

"Nope."

"Then just take hold of him and put him on the ground."

I did so. As soon as I put the rat down, he scooted under the tailpipe and out of sight on the other side of the car.

The shadow withdrew. I heard the front door open. Light gushed out. "'Night, Leo."

◄ What will happen if Cinnamon cleans Leo's other ear? How does Stargirl say that will make her feel?

words for everyday use dis • lodge (dis läj') v., force out of a secure or settled position. *I had to <u>dislodge</u> the rock carefully, as it had been stuck in the crack for a long time.*

"'Night," I called.

I didn't want to leave. I wished I could curl up right there on the driveway and go to sleep. I had been crouching for a long time. It was a chore just to stand. I was halfway home before I could walk right.

Chapter 17

Just two weeks before, I had found out she knew my name, and now I was loopy with love. I was floating. I floated up the white light that washed my sheets and slept on the moon. In school I was a yellow balloon, smiling and lazy, floating above the classrooms. I felt a faint tug on my string. Far below, Kevin was calling, "You're in love, dude!" I merely smiled and rolled over and drifted dreamily out a window.

This state lasted until lunch, when suddenly I became self-conscious. I was certain that everyone in school knew. They would be waiting for me, turning as I entered the lunchroom, staring. I was uncomfortable in the spotlight, always had been. I was happy to stay behind the camera and let Kevin take the bows out front.

So I hid for those thirty-five minutes in the gym equipment room. I sat atop a rolled-up wrestling mat, kicking a volleyball against the opposite wall. I had nothing to eat—I had intended to buy—but I wasn't hungry.

After school we found each other, not that we had to look.

She took Cinnamon from her bag and put him on her shoulder. "Shake paws with Leo, Cinnamon."

Cinnamon and I shook paws.

"Do you believe in enchanted places?" she asked.

"You talking to me or the rat?"

She smiled. She dazzled. "You."

"I don't know," I said. "I never thought about it."

"I'm going to show you one."

"What if I don't want to see it?"

"You think you have a choice?"

She grabbed my hand and almost pulled me off my feet, laughing out loud, and we flew across the school fields, swinging hands for all the world to see.

We walked for miles, out past the business park, MicaTronics, the golf course, into the desert. "Look familiar?" she said.

By now, Cinnamon was riding on my shoulder. And I was carrying the ukulele, strumming nonsense. "It's where we came that day," I said.

◄ *How does Leo feel in the spotlight?*

She gave a snort. "*We? I* was coming out here, *you* were half a mile behind." She poked my shoulder. "*Sneaking* after me." She poked me again, hard this time, but her eyes were twinkling. "*Stalking* me."

I acted horrified, hurt. "Stalking? I was not stalking. I was just lagging behind a little, that's all."

"Following me."

I shrugged. "So?"

"Why?"

I could feel a million reasons, but there were no words to express them. "I don't know."

▶ What does Stargirl say is the reason for Leo following Stargirl to the desert?

"You liked me."

I smiled.

"You were smitten[1] with me. You were speechless to behold my beauty. You had never met anyone so fascinating. You thought of me every waking minute. You dreamed about me. You couldn't stand it. You couldn't let such wonderfulness out of your sight. You *had* to follow me."

I turned to Cinnamon. He licked my nose. "Don't give yourself so much credit. It was your rat I was after."

She laughed, and the desert sang.

To the person who expects every desert to be <u>barren</u> sand dunes, the Sonoran must come as a surprise. Not only are there no dunes, there's no sand. At least not the sort of sand you find at the beach. The ground does have a sandy color to it, or gray, but your feet won't sink in. It's hard, as if it's been tamped. And pebbly. And glinting with—what else— mica.

▶ What do you notice about the Sonoran desert?

But you don't notice the ground much. What you notice are the saguaros. To the newcomer from the East, it's as simple as that. The desert seems to be a brown wasteland of dry, prickly scrub whose only purpose is to serve as a setting for the majestic

---

1. **smitten.** captivated; inspired with feelings of love

words for everyday use bar • ren (băr′ ən) *adj.*, producing inferior or scarce vegetation. *The <u>barren</u> land produced no food to feed the needy families.*

saguaros. Then, little by little, the plants of the desert begin to identify themselves: the porcupiny yucca, the beaver tail and prickly pear and barrel cacti, buckhorn and staghorn and devil's fingers, the tall, sky-reaching tendrils of the ocotillo.

We walked a weaving line around the plant life, up and down washes and gullies, the Maricopas looming lavender in the distance.

"When you turned and ran that day," she said, "I called after you."

"You did?"

"I whispered."

"Whispered? How'd you expect me to hear?"

"I don't know," she said. "I just thought you would."

I strummed the uke. I squared my shoulders. Giving a rat a ride improves the posture.

"You're shy, aren't you?" she said.

"What makes you think that?"

She laughed. "Were you embarrassed when I pulled you along after school today? All those kids looking?"

"Nah."

"Are you lying?"

"Yeah."

She laughed. I seemed to be good at making her laugh.

◀ What does Leo seem to be good at?

I glanced back. The highway was out of sight. "Do you have the time?" I said.

"Nobody has the time," she said. "The time cannot be owned." She threw out her arms and twirled till her multicolored skirt looked like a pinwheel taffy. "The time is free to everyone!"

"Sorry I asked," I said.

She hung her sunflower bag on a cactus arm and cartwheeled toward the Maricopas. Crazily, I felt like joining her. I told myself I couldn't because I was loaded down with a ukulele and a rat. I picked up her bag and followed.

When she decided to walk like a normal human again, I told her she was goofy.

She stopped, turned to me, and bowed grandly. "Thank you, good sir."

Then she took my arm as if we were strolling down a <u>promenade</u> and she said, "Scream, Leo."

"Huh?"

"Just throw your head back and let it all out. Scream your ears off. Nobody will hear you."

"Why would I want to do that?"

She turned her astonished eyes on me. "Why wouldn't you?"

I pointed to Cinnamon. "If he screams first, then I will." And I changed the subject. "Are we ever going to get to this enchanted place?" I felt silly just saying the words.

"Just a little further," she said.

I humored her. "So how do you know an enchanted place when you come to it?"

"You'll see," she said. She squeezed my hand. "Did you know there's a country with officially designated 'enchanted places'?"

"No," I said. "Where would that be? Oz?"

"Iceland."

"Imagine that."

"I'm ignoring your sarcasm. I think it would be neat if we had that here. You'd be walking or riding along, and there would be this stone marker with a brass plate: 'Enchanted Site. U.S. Department of Interior.' "

▶ What does Leo say people would do to the Enchanted Site?

"We'd litter it up," I said.

She stared at me, her smile gone. "Would we?"

I felt bad, as if I had ruined something. "Not really," I told her. "Not if there's a Don't Be a Litterbug sign."

A minute later she stopped. "We're here."

▶ What does Leo first notice about Stargirl's enchanted place?

I looked around. The place couldn't have been more ordinary. The only notable presence was a tall, <u>dilapidated</u> saguaro, a bundle of sticks, in worse shape than Archie's Señor. The rest was gray scrub and tumbleweed and a few prickly pears. "I thought it might look different," I said.

"Special? Scenic?"

---

words for everyday use

prom • e • nade (prä mə nād') *n.*, place for strolling. *The nanny took the baby carriage along the <u>promenade</u>.*

di • lap • i • dat • ed (də la' pə dāt əd) *adj.*, decayed or deteriorated through neglect or misuse. *The <u>dilapidated</u> house plant was sick beyond repair—I was going to have to throw it out.*

"Yeah, I guess."

"It's a different kind of scenery," she said. "Shoes off."

We pulled off our shoes.

"Sit."

We sat, legs crossed. Cinnamon scampered down my arm and onto the ground.

Stargirl shrieked, "Stop!" She scooped up the rat and put him in her bag. "Owls, hawks, snakes. He'd be a tasty meal."

"So," I said, "when does the enchantment start."

We were sitting side by side, facing the mountains.

"It started when the earth was born." Her eyes were closed. Her face was golden in the setting sun. "It never stops. It is, always, It's just here."

"So what do we do?"

She smiled. "That's the secret." Her cupped hands rested in her lap. "We do nothing. Or as close to nothing as we can." Her face turned slowly to me, though her eyes remained closed. "Have you ever done nothing?"

I laughed. "My mother thinks I do it all the time."

"Don't tell her I said so, but your mother is wrong." She turned back to the sun. "It's really hard to do nothing totally. Even just sitting here, like this, our bodies are churning, our minds are chattering. There's a whole commotion going on inside us."

"That's bad?" I said.

"It's bad if we want to know what's going on out-side ourselves."

"Don't we have eyes and ears for that?"

She nodded. "They're okay most of the time. But sometimes they just get in the way. The earth is speaking to us, but we can't hear because of all the racket our senses are making. Sometimes we need to erase them, erase our senses. Then—maybe—the earth will touch us. The universe will speak. The stars will whisper."

The sun was glowing orange now, clipping the mountains' purple crests.

"So how do I become this nothing?"

"I'm not sure," she said. "There's no one answer to that. You have to find your own way. Sometimes I try to erase myself. I imagine a big pink soft soap eraser, and it's going back and forth, back and forth, and it starts down at my toes, back and forth, back and forth, and there they go—poof!—my toes are gone. And then my feet. And then my ankles. But that's the easy part. The hard part is erasing my senses—my eyes, my ears, my nose, my tongue. And last to go is my brain. My thoughts, memories, all the voices inside my head. That's the hardest, erasing my thoughts." She chuckled faintly. "My pumpkin. And then, if I've done a good job, I'm erased. I'm gone. I'm nothing. And then the world is free to flow into me like water into an empty bowl."

▶ What is the hardest part of becoming nothing, according to Stargirl?

"And?" I said.

"And . . . I see. I hear. But not with eyes and ears. I'm not outside my world anymore, and I'm not really inside it either. The thing is, there's no difference anymore between me and the universe. The boundary is gone. I am it and it is me. I am a stone, a cactus thorn. I am rain." She smiled dreamily. "I like that most of all, being rain."

▶ What does Stargirl like being most of all?

"Am I the first one you've brought out here?"

She didn't answer. She faced the mountains, bathed in sun syrup, her face as still and peaceful as I've ever seen a face.

"Stargirl—"

"Shhhh."

That was the last sound either of us made for a long time. We sat side by side, lotus style,[2] facing west. I closed my eyes. I tried to be perfectly still—and promptly found out that she was right. I could <u>immobilize</u> my arms and legs, but inside me it was rush hour in downtown Phoenix. I had never been so aware of my breath and my heartbeat, not to mention other assorted grumblings and gurglings. And my head—it just wouldn't close down. Every ques-

---

2. **lotus style.** Cross-legged sitting position.

---

words for everyday use   im • mob • i • lize (i mō′ bə līz′) v., reduce or eliminate motion of the body or a body part. *After sitting on my feet for an hour, I was <u>immobilized</u> from the knees down.*

tion, every stray thought from miles around came wandering into my brain, sniffing about, scratching at my attention.

But I tried. I tried the eraser, but it wouldn't even wipe out the first toe. I tried to imagine I was sawdust blowing away with the wind. Swallowed by a whale. Dissolving away like Alka-Seltzer. Nothing worked. I could not make myself disappear.

I peeked. I knew I wasn't supposed to, but I did. Clearly, she had erased herself. She was gone. She was serenity. Her lips faintly smiling. Her golden skin. The glowing threadends of her hair. She seemed to have been dipped in sunlight and set here to dry. I felt a pang of jealousy, that she could be sitting next to me and not know it. That she could be somewhere most wonderful and I could not be there, too.

Then I saw the rat. He had crawled out of the bag. He was sitting on it much as we were, his front paws—I kept thinking of them as tiny hands, they were so human-like—dangling before him. He, too, was not moving. He, too, was facing the sunset, his pelt the color of a new penny. His peppercorn eyes were fully open.

I knew it must have been a trick she had taught him, or imitative rodent behavior. Still, I couldn't help thinking there was more to it, that the whiskered little fellow was having an experience of his own—which might include digestion in a critter's stomach if Stargirl's fears came true. As quietly as possible, I reached over and scooped him up. I held him in both hands. He did not struggle or squirm, but resumed facing the sunset with his tiny chin resting on my forefinger. In my fingertips I could feel his heartbeat. I drew him closer to my chest. I dared any varmint to come near.

◀ *What does Leo do to Cinnamon when he comes out of the bag?*

I took a deep breath and closed my eyes for another try at enchantment. I don't think I succeeded. I think Cinnamon was a better eraser than I. I tried. I tried so hard I almost squeaked, but I could not seem to leave myself, and the cosmos did not visit me. I could not stop wondering what time it was.

But something did happen. A small thing. I was aware of stepping over a line, of taking one step into territory new to me. It was a territory of peace, of silence. I had never experienced such utter silence before, such stillness. The commotion within me went on, but at a lower volume, as if someone had turned down my dial. And an eerie thing happened. While I never did totally lose awareness of myself, I believe I did, so to speak, lose Cinnamon. I no longer felt his pulse, his presence, in my hands. It seemed we were no longer separate, but were one.

When the sun fell behind the mountains, I felt it as a faint coolness on my face.

I don't know how long my eyes were closed. When I opened them, she was gone. Alarmed, I jerked around. She was standing off a ways, smiling. Evening had come. While my eyes were closed, the mountains' dusky lavender had drifted over the desert.

We put on our shoes. We headed for the highway. I expected her to <u>interrogate</u> me, but she did not. One moment the moon was not there, and then it was, then one bright star. We walked across the desert hand in hand, saying nothing.

▶ *What do Leo and Stargirl talk about as they leave the enchanted place?*

words for everyday use

in • ter • ro • gate (in ter′ ə gāt′) v., ask questions of. *I knew my mom would <u>interrogate</u> me when I arrived home two hours late.*

Chapter 18

We were alone. We were the only ones in school.

At least that's how it seemed in the following days.

As I went about my day, I felt her going about hers. I sensed her movement, her presence in distant parts of the building. Walking the halls between classes, I didn't have to see her, I knew she was there: unseen in the mob heading my way, about to turn a corner five classroom doors down. I homed in[1] on the beacon[2] of her smile. As we approached each other, the noise and the students around us melted away and we were utterly alone, passing, smiling, holding each other's eyes, floors and walls gone, two people in a universe of space and stars.

And then one day I began to discover that we were more alone than I had dreamed.

It was a Thursday. Normally on that day, after third period, Stargirl and I would pass each other on the second floor around the teachers' lounge. We would smile and say hi and continue on our way to our separate classes. On this day, <u>impulsively</u>, I fell in alongside her.

"How about an escort?" I said.

She grinned slyly. "Anybody in mind?"

We touched little fingers and walked on. Her next class was on the first floor, so we went down the nearest stairway. We were walking side by side. That's when I noticed.

◀ *What does Leo notice about the other students at MAHS?*

No one spoke to us.

No one nodded to us.

No one smiled at us.

No one looked at us.

A crowded stairway, and no shoulder, no sleeve brushed us.

---

1. **homed in.** Direct attention toward an objective
2. **beacon.** Light

---

words for everyday use   im • pul • sive (im pəl′ siv) *adj.*, spontaneous. *Although Juan used to be a very thoughtful shopper, he has become very <u>impulsive</u> in his spending.* **impulsively,** *adv.*

Students climbing the steps veered to the railing or wall. Except for Stargirl jabbering in my ear, the usual raucous chatter was absent.

Mostly what I noticed were the eyes. Faces turned up from the steps below, but the eyes never connected with us. They went right on through us as if they were gamma rays.[3] Or they nipped our ears and rattled off among the walls and other eyes. I had an urge to look down at myself, to make sure I was there.

At lunch I said to Kevin, "Nobody looks at me."

He was staring at his sandwich.

"Kevin!" I snapped. "Now *you're* doing it."

He came up laughing. He looked me square in the eyes. "Sorry."

Usually there were others at the table. Today there was only us. I leaned across my lunch. "Kevin, what's going on?"

▶ What had Kevin been hoping Leo wouldn't notice?

He looked off, then back to me. "I was wondering when you'd notice. Kinda hoping you wouldn't."

"Notice *what?*"

He stalled by taking a bite of tuna salad sandwich. He took his time chewing. He drank orangeade[4] from a straw. "First of all, it's not you."

I pulled back. I held out my hands. "It's not me. What's that supposed to mean?"

"It's who you're with."

I sat there, blinking, staring at him. "Stargirl?"

He nodded.

"Okay," I said. "So?"

He stared at me some more, chewed, swallowed, sipped, looked away, looked back. "They're not talking to her."

The words didn't stick. "What do you mean? Who's 'they'?"

He cocked his head at the sea of tables and eaters. "Them."

"Who them?" I said, too unhinged to laugh at my grammar.

He wet his lips. "All of them." He shrugged. "Well, almost." His eyes drifted over my shoulder. "There're still two girls sitting with her."

---

3. **gamma rays.** Electromagnetic radiation, similar to x-rays
4. **orangeade.** An orange-flavored soft drink

I glanced back. At the height of Stargirl's popularity, kids had been pulling chairs from other tables to squeeze around hers. Now it was just Stargirl, Dori Dilson, and a ninth-grader.

"So," I said, "exactly what is going on?"

He sipped from his straw. "The silent treatment is going on. Nobody's talking to her."

◀ What does Kevin say is going on?

It still wasn't sticking. "What do you mean, 'nobody's talking to her'? What, did everybody have a meeting in the gym and vote on it?"

"It wasn't that official. It just happened. Got up steam."

I gaped at him. "When? When did it start? How? Why?" I was beginning to screech.

"I don't know exactly. After the basketball stuff, I guess. That really ticked off a lot of people."

◀ When does Kevin say this treatment started?

"The basketball stuff."

He nodded.

"The basketball stuff," I repeated dumbly.

He put down his sandwich. "Leo, don't act like you don't know what I'm talking about. Cheering for the other team? What did you think, people thought that was *cute?*"

"It was her, Kevin. It was harmless. Weird maybe, but harmless. It was *her.*"

He nodded slowly. "Yeah, well, I guess that's what I'm saying. It's not just one thing she did. It's everything. Don't tell me you never noticed. Remember a certain tomato?"

"Kevin, a couple of months ago everybody stood and cheered in the auditorium when she won the oratorical contest."

"Hey"—he gestured defensively—"tell *them.*"

"One person threw the tomato. One."

Kevin snickered. "Yeah, and a thousand wanted to. Did you notice the cheers when it happened? People blame her. For the team losing. For our undefeated season going down the toilet."

---

words for everyday use   gape (gāp) v., gaze stupidly or in openmouthed surprise or wonder. *When I heard the results, all I could do was gape in utter astonishment.*

I wasn't sure Kevin was still talking about "them."

"Kevin—" I felt myself pleading. "She was only a *cheerleader.*"

"Leo"—he was pointing—"you asked me what was going on, I told you." He stood up and took his tray to the belt.

I stared at his empty chair until he returned.

"Kevin . . . the Happy Birthday songs, the Valentine cards, all the nice things she does for people . . . doesn't that count for something?"

The bell rang.

He got up. He gathered his books. He shrugged. "I guess not."

▶ What happens to Leo over the next few days?

For the rest of the day, and the next and the next, I grew increasingly paranoid. Walking with her in and around the school, I was intensely aware that the nature of our aloneness had changed. It was no longer a cozy, tunnel-of-love sweetness, but a chilling isolation. We never had to veer, never had to make way for someone else; everyone made way for us. Hallway crowds fell away from us. Except for Hillari Kimble. Whenever we passed her, she tilted toward us with a gloating smirk on her face.

As for Stargirl, she didn't seem to notice. She jabbered constantly in my ear. While I smiled and nodded to her, frost formed on the back of my neck.

words for everyday use

is • o • la • tion (ī' sə lā' shən) *n.,* condition of being apart from others. *The doctor recommended she remain in isolation until they were certain she was not contagious.*

Chapter 19

"The Amish in Pennsylvania have a word for it."

"What's that?" I said.

"Shunning."

I was at Archie's. I had to talk to someone.

"Well, that's what's happening."

"The shunnee, so to speak, has gotten himself in dutch with the church, so he's excommunicated.[1] The whole community is in on it. Unless he repents, nobody speaks to him for the rest of his life. Not even his family."

"What?!"

"That's right. Not even his family."

"What about his wife?"

"Wife. Kids. Everybody." His pipe had gone out. He relit it with a stick match. "I believe the idea is to drive him away. But some stay, continue working the farm, having dinner. If he passes the salt to his wife, she ignores it. If the bishop had his way, the pigs and chickens would ignore him. It's as if he doesn't exist."

I nodded. "I know the feeling."

We were on the back porch. I stared out at Señor Saguaro.

He said, "Does it happen to you when you're not with her?"

◀ Does Leo think he's being ignored when he's not with Stargirl?

"No," I said. "At least I don't think so. But when I'm with her, I feel like it's aimed at me, too."

A small pipe cloud left the corner of his mouth. He smiled sadly. "Poor dolphin. Caught in a tuna net."

I picked up Barney, the Paleocene rodent skull. I wondered if someone would be holding Cinnamon's head 60 million years from now. "So, what should I do?"

---

1. **excommunicated.** Excluded; kicked out

words for everyday use	shun (shən') v., avoid deliberately. *Matt did not want to speak to or come in contact with Dylan, so Matt shunned him.* re • pent (ri pent') v., feel regret or	change one's mind; turn from sin. *Realizing that going through with the ceremony was not really what I should be doing, I repented and declined.*

Archie waved his hand. "Oh, well, that's the easy part. Stay away from her: your problem's *kaput.*"

I sneered. "Great advice. You know it's not that easy."

He did know, of course, but he wanted me to say it. I told him about the valentine, the night in her driveway, the walk in the desert. The question that came to mind then sounded silly, but it persisted: "Do you believe in enchanted places?"

He took the pipe from his mouth and looked straight at me. "Absolutely."

I was confused. "But you're a scientist. A man of science."

▶ What is Archie's explanation for why he believes in enchanted places?

"A man of bones. You can't be up to your eyeballs in bones and not believe in enchanted places."

I looked at Barney. I ran my fingertip along the hard line of his two-inch jaw, rough like a cat's tongue. Sixty million years in my hands. I looked at Archie. "Why can't she be . . ."

He finished for me: ". . . like everybody else?"

He stood up and stepped down from the porch onto the desert—for his back yard, except for the shed where he kept his digging tools, *was* the desert. Nature did the landscaping. I put down Barney and joined him. We <u>ambled</u> toward Señor Saguaro.

"Not like everybody else," I said. "Not exactly. Not totally. But . . . Archie . . ." I stopped. He stopped. I turned full-face to him. My thoughts and feelings were a wild, conflicting jumble. After staring stupidly at him for a long time, I blurted, "She cheers for the other team!"

Archie pulled the pipe from his mouth, as if to better digest my words. He raised one finger in the air. He nodded solemnly. "Ahh, yes."

We resumed walking.

We walked on past the toolshed, past Señor Saguaro. Occasionally I picked up a stone and flung it toward the purple Maricopas.

---

words for everyday use

am • ble (am' bəl) v., go at an easy pace; saunter. *I ambled through town, not caring what time I got home.*

Archie said, almost in a whisper, "She's not easy to put into words, is she?"

I shook my head.

"An unusual girl," he said. "Could see that from the first. And her parents, as ordinary, in a nice way, as could be. How did this girl come to be? I used to ask myself. Sometimes I thought she should be teaching me. She seems to be in touch with something that the rest of us are missing." He looked at me. "Hm?"

◄ How does Archie describe Stargirl's parents?

I nodded.

He turned the mahogany[2] bowl of his pipe upside down and rapped it with his knuckle. A small stream of ash spilled onto a thicket of dead mesquite.[3]

He pointed the pipe stem at me. "You know, there's a place we all inhabit, but we don't much think about it, we're <u>scarcely</u> conscious of it, and it lasts for less than a minute a day."

"What's that?" I said.

"It's in the morning, for most of us. It's that time, those few seconds when we're coming out of sleep but we're not really awake yet. For those few seconds we're something more primitive than what we are about to become. We have just slept the sleep of our most distant ancestors, and something of them and their world still clings to us. For those few moments we are unformed, uncivilized. We are not the people we know as ourselves, but creatures more in tune with a tree than a keyboard. We are untitled, unnamed, natural, suspended between was and will be, the tadpole before the frog, the worm before the butterfly. We are, for a few brief moments, anything and everything we could be. And then . . ."

He pulled out his pouch and repacked his pipe. Cherryscent flew. He struck a match. The pipe bowl, like some predator, or seducer, drew down the flame.

---

2. **mahogany.** Reddish-brown wood
3. **thicket of dead mesquite.** Groups of trees or shrubs that are found in the southwestern area of the United States

words for everyday use
scarce • ly (skers' lē) adv., almost not. There was <u>scarcely</u> enough room for Harris to fit in the already crowded car, but he managed.

▶ How does Leo
describe what
happens to Archie's
words?

". . . and then—ah—we open our eyes and the day is before us, and"—he snapped his fingers—"we become ourselves."

Like so many of Archie's words, they seemed not to enter through my ears but to settle on my skin, there to burrow like tiny eggs awaiting the rain of my maturity, when they would hatch and I at last would understand.

We walked in silence. Yellow blooms had appeared on a cactus, and for some reason that made me incredibly sad. The purple of the mountains flowed like watercolor.

"They *hate* her," I said.

He stopped. He looked <u>intently</u> at me. He turned me around and we headed back. He put his arm around my shoulder. "Let's consult Señor Saguaro."

Shortly we were standing before the <u>derelict</u> giant. I never understood how the Señor managed to convey a sense of dignity, majesty even, considering his stick-rickety, see-through skeleton and the ridiculous, leathery crumple of hide about his foot, his fallen britches. Archie always spoke to him with respectful formality, as to a judge or visiting dignitary.

"Good day, Señor Saguaro," he began. "I believe you know my friend and charter member of the Loyal Order of the Stone Bone, Mr. Borlock." He whispered an aside to me: "I'm a little rusty, but I think I'll use Spanish now. He prefers it on delicate matters." He turned back to the cactus. *"Parece, Señor Borlock aquí es la víctima de un 'shunning' de sus compañeros estudiantes en el liceo. El objeto principal del 'shunning' es la enamorada del Señor Borlock, nuestra propia Señorita Niña Estrella. El está en búsqueda de preguntas."* [4]

---

4. *"Parece, Señor Borlock . . . preguntas."* Spanish: "It seems, Mr. Borlock here is the victim of 'shunning' by his classmates. The main objective of 'shunning' is Mr. Borlock's girlfriend, our own Stargirl. He is in search of questions."

**words
for
everyday
use**

in • tent (in tent') *adj.*, earnest, fixed. *Her* <u>*intent*</u> *stare made me uneasy.* **intently,** *adv.*

der • e • lict (der' ə likt) *adj.*, abandoned. *In cleaning my room, I discovered my* <u>*derelict*</u> *bear; I hadn't played with it in years.*

As Archie spoke, he looked up toward the elf owl hole. Now he turned back to me and whispered, "I asked for questions."

"Questions?" I whispered. "What about answers?"

But he was turning from me, tilting his head toward the great cactus, his finger on his lips— "Shh"—his eyes closed.

I waited.

At last he nodded and turned back to me. "The <u>esteemed</u> Señor says there is only one question."

"What's that?" I said.

"He says it all boils down to this—if I'm translating correctly: Whose affection do you value more, hers or the others'? The Señor says everything will follow from that."

I wasn't sure I understood the Señor any more than I understood Archie half the time, but I said nothing, and I went home. In bed that night, as the moonlight reached high tide under my chin, I realized that in fact I understood the question perfectly. I just didn't want to answer it.

◀ Where does Archie look while he's talking?

words for everyday use   es • teem (is tēm') *n.*, high regard. *Because of our <u>esteem</u> for Dr. Randell, we presented him with an award.* esteemed, *adj.*

Chapter 20

Twice a week the results of the state basketball tournament were posted on the plywood roadrunner in the courtyard. The surviving teams were into the sectionals now; then would come the regionals; then, with only two teams left, the big show, the Arizona state championship. Glendale, the team we had lost to, got bitter, <u>masochistic</u> attention on the roadrunner with scores in foot-high numerals, as they continued to win and move through the tournament.

▶ What tournament is Stargirl involved in?

Meanwhile, Stargirl was involved in a tournament of her own, the oratorical contest. As Mica High's winner, she qualified for the district "talk-off," as the *Times* called it. It took place in the auditorium of Red Rock High School, and lo and behold, Stargirl won that, too. Next stop was the state finals in Phoenix on the third Friday in April.

In my homeroom, when the announcement came over the PA about Stargirl winning the district title, I was about to let out a cheer, but I caught myself. Several people booed.

Getting ready for the finals, Stargirl practiced on me. Most often we went into the desert. She did not use notes, nor did her words seem memorized. Each time she gave the speech, it was different. She seemed to insert new material as it popped into her head. She matched her words so perfectly that the speech was not a speech at all, but one creature's voice in the wild, as natural as a raven's caw or a coyote's howl at midnight.

I sat cross-legged on the ground, Cinnamon sat on me. We listened in <u>rapture</u>, and so, I half believed, did the tumbleweed and cacti, the desert, the mountains, all listening to the girl in the longfalling skirt. What a shame, I thought, to pack her performance into a schedule and present it to rows of plush-back seats in an auditorium. Once, incredibly, an elf owl

---

words for everyday use

mas • o • chis • tic (ma' sə kis' tik) *adj.,* quality of taking pleasure in suffering. *The masochistic bully enjoyed hurting his classmates during recess.*

rap • ture (rap' chər) *n.,* great pleasure. *The audience listened to the great pianist in complete rapture.*

landed atop a saguaro not ten feet from where she was speaking. It paused for a full minute before ducking into its hole.

Of course, we did other things, too. We walked. We talked. We rode bikes. Though I had my driver's license, I bought a cheap secondhand bicycle so I could ride with her. Sometimes she led the way, sometimes I did. Whenever we could, we rode side by side.

She was bendable light: she shone around every corner of my day.

She taught me to <u>revel</u>. She taught me to wonder. She taught me to laugh. My sense of humor had always measured up to everyone else's; but timid, <u>introverted</u> me, I showed it sparingly: I was a smiler. In her presence I threw back my head and laughed out loud for the first time in my life.

◄ How has Leo's laugh changed since spending time with Stargirl?

She saw things. I had not known there was so much to see.

She was forever tugging my arm and saying, "Look!"

I would look around, seeing nothing. "Where?"

She would point. "There."

In the beginning I still could not see. She might be pointing to a doorway, or a person, or the sky. But such things were so common to my eyes, so undistinguished, that they would register as "nothing." I walked in a gray world of nothings.

So she would stop and point out that the front door of the house we were passing was blue. And that the last time we had passed it, it had been green. And that as near as she could tell, someone who lived in that house painted the front door a different color several times a year.

Or she would whisper to me that the old man sitting alone on the bench at the Tudor Village shopping center was holding his hearing aid in his hand, and he was smiling, and he wore a coat and tie as if

| words for everyday use | **rev • el** (re' vəl) v., take immense pleasure. *He reveled in the spotlight; he was meant to be there.* | **in • tro • vert** (in' trə vərt') n., reserved or shy person. *My brother is an introvert, so I help him try to overcome some of his shyness.* |

he were going somewhere special, and pinned onto his lapel was a tiny American flag.

Or she would kneel down and pull me down with her and show me the ants, two of them, lugging the lopped leg of a beetle twenty times their size across the sidewalk, as might two men, were they strong as ants, carry a full-grown tree from one end of town to the other.

After a while I began to see better. When she said "Look!" and I followed her pointing finger, I saw. Eventually it became a contest: who would see first? When I finally did it—said "Look!" and pointed and tugged *her* sleeve—I was as proud as a first-grader with a star on his paper.

▶ How does Stargirl see differently than most people?

And there was more to her seeing than that. What she saw, she felt. Her eyes went straight to her heart. The old man on the bench, for example, made her cry. The lumberjack ants made her laugh. The door of many colors put her in such a snit of curiosity that I had to drag her away; she felt she could not proceed with her life until she knocked on such a door.

She told me how she would run the *Mica Times* if she were the editor. Crime would be on page 10, ants and old men and painted doors on page 1. She made up headlines:

ANTS HAUL MONSTER LOAD
ACROSS VAST, BARREN WALK

MYSTERY SMILE: OLD MAN
NODS OFF AT TUDOR VILLAGE

DOOR BEGS: KNOCK ME!

▶ What does Stargirl want to do for her career in the future?

I told her I wanted to be a TV director. She said she wanted to be a silver-lunch-truck driver.

"Huh?" I said.

"You know," she said. "people work all morning and then it's twelve o'clock. The secretaries in the offices walk out the door, the construction workers put down their hard hats and hammers, and everybody's hungry, and they look up and there I am! No matter where they are, no matter where they work,

I'm there. I have a whole fleet of silver lunch trucks. They go everywhere. 'Let Lunch Come to You!' That's my slogan. Just seeing my silver lunch truck makes them happy." She described how she would roll up the side panels and everyone would practically faint at the cloud of wonderful smells. Hot food, cold food, Chinese, Italian, you name it. Even a salad bar. "They can't believe how much food I fit into my truck. No matter where you are—out in the desert, the mountains, even down in the mines—if you want my silver lunch service, I get it to you. I find a way."

I tagged along on missions. One day she bought a small plant, an African violet in a plastic pot on sale for ninety-nine cents at a drugstore.

◀ What does Stargirl buy at a drugstore? Who does she say it's for?

"Who's it for?" I asked her.

"I'm not exactly sure," she said. "I just know that someone at an address on Marion Drive is in the hospital for surgery, so I thought whoever's back home could use a little cheering up."

"How do you know this stuff?" I said.

She gave me a mischievous grin. "I have my ways."

We went to the house on Marion Drive. She reached into the saddle pack behind her bicycle seat. She pulled out a handful of ribbons. She chose a pale violet one that matched the color of the tiny blossoms and stuffed the remaining ribbons back into the seat pack. She tied the violet ribbon around the pot. I held her bike while she set the plant by the front door.

Riding away, I said, "Why don't you leave a card or something with your name on it?"

The question surprised her. "Why should I?"

Her question surprised me. "Well, I don't know, it's just the way people do things. They expect it. They get a gift, they expect to know where it came from."

"Is that important?"

"Yeah, I guess—"

I never finished that thought. My tires shuddered as I slammed my bike to a halt. She stopped ahead of me. She backed up. She stared.

"Leo, what is it?"

I wagged my head. I grinned. I pointed to her. "It was *you*."

"Me what?"

"Two years ago. My birthday. I found a package on my front step. A porcupine necktie. I never found out who gave it to me."

She walked her bike alongside mine. She grinned. "A mystery."

"Where did you find it?" I said.

"I didn't. I had my mother make it."

▶ Who made the porcupine necktie that Stargirl left for Leo two years ago?

She didn't seem to want to dwell on the subject. She started pedaling and we continued on our way.

"Where were we?" she said.

"Getting credit," I said.

"What about it?"

"Well, it's nice to get credit."

The spokes of her rear wheel spun behind the curtain of her long skirt. She looked like a photograph from a hundred years ago. She turned her wide eyes on me. "Is it?" she said.

Chapter 21

On weekends and after dinner, we delivered many potted violets. And CONGRATULATIONS! balloons. And cards of many sentiments. She made her own cards. She wasn't a great artist. Her people were stick figures. The girls all had triangle skirts and pigtails. You would never mistake one of her cards for a Hallmark, but I have never seen cards more heartfelt. They were meaningful in the way that a schoolchild's homemade Christmas card is meaningful. She never left her name.

But finally, after much pestering from me, she did tell me how she knew what was going on in people's lives. It was simple, she said. She read the daily paper. Not the headlines or the front page or the sports page or the comics or the TV listings or the Hollywood gossip. What she read were the parts that most people ignored, the parts without headlines and pictures, the <u>boondocks</u> of the paper: the hospital admissions, the death notices, the birthday and wedding announcements, the police blotter, the coming events calendar.

How does Stargirl know what is going on in people's lives?

Most of all, she read the fillers.

"I *love* fillers!" she exclaimed.

"What are fillers?" I said.

She explained that fillers are little items that are not considered important enough to be a story or to have a headline. They're never more than one column wide, never more than an inch or two deep. They are most commonly found at the bottoms of inside pages, where the eye seldom travels. If the editors had their way, they would never use fillers. But sometimes a reporter doesn't write quite enough words, and the story doesn't reach all the way to the bottom of the page. The paper can't have a blank space there, so the editor dumps in a filler. A filler doesn't need to be "news." It doesn't need to be

What is the purpose of a filler?

---

words for everyday use   **boon • docks** (bün′ däks) *n.*, rough country filled with dense brush. *We drove so far out of the city we ended up in the* <u>boondocks</u> *with nothing in sight for miles.*

important. It doesn't even need to be read. All it's asked to do is take up space.

A filler might come from anywhere and be about anything. It might tell how many pounds of rice a typical Chinese person eats in a lifetime. Or say something about beetles in Sumatra. Or the filler might come from down the street. It might mention that so-and-so's cat is missing. Or that so-and-so has a collection of antique marbles.

"I search through fillers like a prospector digging for gold," she said.

"So that's it?" I said. "You read the papers?"

"No," she said, "that's not all. There's also the place where I get my hair cut. I always overhear good stuff there. And of course there're bulletin boards. Do you know how many bulletin boards there are in town?"

"Sure," I said <u>facetiously</u>, "I count them every day."

"So do I," she said, not kidding. "So far, I'm up to forty-one."

Offhand, I couldn't think of one, except the plywood roadrunner. "What do you learn from bulletin boards?"

"Oh . . . somebody just opened a business. Somebody lost a dog. Somebody needs a companion."

"Who advertises for a companion?" I said. "Who needs one that bad?"

"Lonely people," she said. "Old people. Just somebody to sit with them for a while."

I pictured Stargirl sitting in a dark room with an old woman. I couldn't picture myself doing the same thing. Sometimes she seemed so far from me.

We were passing Pisa Pizza. "There's a bulletin board in there," she said.

It was just inside the door. It was smothered with business cards and notices. I pointed to one that said "Odd Jobs—Ask for Mike," call this number. "So

---

words for everyday use **fac • e • tious** (fə sē′ shəs) adj., witty in a playful but often inappropriate manner. *I knew that Rita was being <u>facetious</u> when she remarked that Kristin's new hair color was like a ripe pumpkin, but Kristin's feelings were hurt.* **facetiously,** adv.

what's that tell you?" I said, with more challenge in my voice than I intended.

She read it. "Well, it could be that Mike lost his regular job and can't find another, so he's hiring himself out. Or even if he has a regular job, it's not enough to make ends meet. He's either not very neat, or he can't afford a whole piece of paper. This is just a scrap."

"So what would you do for him?" I said.

"Oh, I don't know. My parents might have an odd job they need done. Or maybe I do. Or maybe I could just send him a card."

"What kind of card would he get?"

"A Keep-your-chin-up card." She poked me. "Hey, want to play a card game?"

I had a feeling she wasn't talking about poker. "Sure," I said.

She said she invented it. "All you need is your eyes and one other person. I pick somebody on the street, the mall, a store, wherever, and I follow them. Say it's a her. I follow her for fifteen minutes, not a minute more. I time myself. The game is, after fifteen minutes of watching her, I have to guess what kind of card she needs."

"But how can you get it to her?" I said. "You don't know where she lives."

"True. That's as far as it goes. That's why it's just a game. It's just for fun." She snuggled into me. She whispered in my ear, "Let's play."

I said sure.

She said we needed a mall. I usually steered us away from the Mica Mall—too many silent-treatment MAHS kids hanging around there. We drove ten miles to the Redstone Mall. It was a Saturday afternoon.

We picked out a woman. Lime-green skort.[1] White sandals. We guessed her age was early forties. She was buying a soft pretzel—regular, salted—at Auntie Anne's. She carried the pretzel in a little white paper bag. We followed her into Suncoast Video. We overheard her ask for *When Harry Met Sally*. They didn't

◀ *What does Stargirl think she might do for Mike?*

◀ *Why does Leo stay clear of the Mica Mall?*

---

1. **skort.** Women's clothing item that combines shorts and skirt

have it. She passed Sonoma, then came back and went in. She wandered about, touching pottery with one fingertip, feeling surfaces. She stopped before the dinner plates. She lifted one with a French café painted on it. "Van Gogh," Stargirl whispered. The lady seemed to think about the plate, even closed her eyes, holding it to her chest with both hands, as if feeling vibrations. But then she put it back and walked out. On to Sears. Lingerie. Bedclothes. I was uneasy, spying from behind a rack of frilly some-things. She was flipping through nightshirts when time ran out.

Stargirl and I <u>conferred</u> in the corridor.

"Okay," she said, "what do you think?"

"I think I feel like a stalker," I said.

"A good stalker," she said.

"You first," I said.

"Well, she's divorced and lonely. No wedding ring. Wants somebody in her life. A home life. She wishes she were Sally and her Harry would come along. She would make him dinner and snuggle with him at night. She tries to eat low-fat foods. She works for a travel agency. She took a free cruise last year, but all she met on the boat were creeps. Her name is Clarissa, she played the clarinet in high school, and her favorite soap is Irish Spring."

I boggled. "How do you know all that?"

She laughed. "I don't. I'm guessing. That's what makes it fun."

"So what card would you send her?"

She put her finger to her lips. "Hmm . . . to Clarissa I would send a While-you're-waiting-for-Harry-be-good-to-yourself card. How about you?"

"I would send a"—I <u>mulled</u> over the phrasing—"a Don't-let-Harry-catch-you-flicking card."

Now it was her turn to boggle. "Huh?"

"Didn't you see her pick her nose?" I said. "In Suncoast?"

words for everyday use

con • fer (kən fer') v., meet for discussion; have a conference. *Mom and Dad <u>conferred</u> before letting me have the car for the evening.*

mull (məl') v., consider at length; ponder. *After a week of <u>mulling</u> over which classes to take, I finally made my decision and turned in my registration.*

"Not really. I saw her hand go to her nose, like she was scratching it or something."

"Yeah, or something. She was picking, that's what. She was quick and sneaky. A real pro."

She gave me a playful shove. "You're kidding."

I held up my hands. "I'm serious. She was standing in front of the comedies. Her finger went in and when it came out there was something on it. She carried it around for about a minute. And then, just as she was leaving Suncoast, when she thought nobody was looking, she flicked. I didn't see where it landed." She stared at me. I raised my right hand and put my left over my heart. "No lie."

She broke out laughing, so loudly I was embarrassed. She grabbed my arm with both hands to keep from collapsing. Mallwalkers stared.

We carded two others that day: a woman who spent her whole fifteen minutes feeling leather jackets—we called her Betty—and a man we called Adam because of his huge Adam's apple, which we renamed Adam's pumpkin. No more pick-'n'-flickers.

And I did have fun. Whether it came from the game or simply from being with her, I don't know. I do know I was surprised at how close I felt to Clarissa and Betty and Adam after watching them for only fifteen minutes.

Throughout the day, Stargirl had been dropping money. She was the Johnny Appleseed of loose change: a penny here, a nickel there. Tossed to the sidewalk, laid on a shelf or bench. Even quarters.

◀ *What had Stargirl been doing throughout the day?*

"I hate change," she said. "It's so . . . jangly."

"Do you realize how much you must throw away in a year?" I said.

"Did you ever see a little kid's face when he spots a penny on a sidewalk?" she said.

When her change purse was empty, we drove back to Mica. Along the way she invited me to dinner at her house.

Chapter 22

Archie had claimed the Caraways were normal folks, but I still couldn't imagine Stargirl coming from an ordinary home. I think I expected a leftover hippie scene from the 1960s. Make love, not war. Her mother in a long skirt with a flower in her hair. Her father's face framed in muttonchop sideburns,[1] saying "Groovy!" and "Right on!" a lot. Grateful Dead posters. Psychedelic lampshades.

So I was surprised. Her mother wore shorts and a tank top as she worked the pedal of a sewing machine with her bare foot. She was making a Russian peasant costume for a play to be presented in Denver. Mr. Caraway was on a stepladder outside, painting windowsills. No muttonchops; in fact, not much hair at all. The house itself could have been anyone's. Glossy bentwood furniture, throw rugs over hardwood floors, Southwest accents: an Anasazi-style[2] wedding vase here, a Georgia O'Keeffe[3] print there. Nothing to <u>proclaim</u>, "You see? She came from *here*."

▶ What is Stargirl's mother making?

Same with her room. Except for Cinnamon's blue and yellow plywood apartment in one corner, it might have belonged to any high school girl. I stood in the doorway.

"What?" she asked.

"I'm surprised," I said.

"At what?"

"I thought your room would be different."

"How so?"

"I don't know. More . . . you."

She grinned. "Stacks of fillers? A card-making operation?"

"Something like that."

---

1. **muttonchop sideburns**. Side-whiskers that are narrow at the temple and broad and round by the lower jaws
2. **Anasazi-style**. Relating to prehistoric American Indians of Northern Arizona and New Mexico
3. **Georgia O'Keeffe**. American painter

words for everyday use pro • claim (prō klām′) *v.*, announce. *After the dinner dishes were cleared, my mother <u>proclaimed</u> the rest of the evening was to be spent addressing envelopes for the party.*

"That's my office," she said. She let Cinnamon out. He scurried under her bed. "This is my room."

"You have an office?"

"Yep." She stuck her foot under the bed. When it came out, Cinnamon was aboard. "I wanted to have a place all my own where I could go to work. So I got one.

Cinnamon scampered out of the room.

"Where is it?" I said.

She put her finger to her lips. "Secret."

"Bet I know one person who knows," I said.

She raised her eyebrows.

"Archie."

She smiled.

"He was talking about you," I said. "He likes you."

"He means the world to me," she said. "I think of him as my grandfather."

My inspection yielded two curious items. One was a wooden bowl half filled with sand-colored hair.

"Yours?" I said.

She nodded. "For birds looking for nest materials. I put it out in the spring. Been doing it since I was a little girl. I got more business up north than here."

The other item was on a bookshelf. It was a tiny wagon about the size of my fist. It was made of wood and looked like it might have been an antique toy. It was piled high with pebbles. Several other pebbles lay about the wagon wheels.

I pointed to it. "You collecting stones, or what?"

"It's my happy wagon," she said. "Actually, it could just as well be called an unhappy wagon, but I prefer happy."

"So what's it all about?"

"It's about how I feel. When something makes me happy, I put a pebble in the wagon. If I'm unhappy, I take a pebble out. There are twenty pebbles in all."

I counted three on the shelf. "So there're seventeen in the wagon now, right?"

"Right."

"So that means, what, you're pretty happy?"

"Right again."

"What's the biggest number of pebbles ever in the wagon?"

◀ Who does Leo think knows about the location of Stargirl's office?

◀ What's the biggest number of pebbles Stargirl has ever had in her wagon?

She gave me a sly smile. "You're looking at it."

It didn't seem like just a pile of pebbles anymore.

"Usually," she said, "it's more balanced. It hangs around ten, a couple to one side or the other. Back and forth, back and forth. Like life."

"How close to empty did the wagon ever get?" I said.

"Oh . . ." She turned her face to the ceiling, closed her eyes. "Once, down to three."

I was shocked. "Really? You?"

She stared. "Why *not* me?"

"You don't seem the type."

"What type is that?"

"I don't know . . ." I groped for the right words.

"The three-pebble type?" she offered.

I shrugged.

She picked up a pebble from the shelf and, with a grin, dropped it into the wagon. "Well, call me Miss Unpredictable."

I joined the family for dinner. Three of us had meatloaf. The fourth—guess who—was a strict vegetarian. She had tofu loaf.

▶ *What did Stargirl eat for dinner?*

Her parents called her "Stargirl" and "Star" as casually as if she were a Jennifer.

After dinner we sat on her front step. She had brought her camera out. Three little kids, two girls and a boy, were playing in a driveway across the street. She took several pictures of them.

"Why are you doing that?" I asked her.

"See the little boy in the red cap?" she said. "His name is Peter Sinkowitz. He's five years old. I'm doing his biography, sort of."

For the tenth time that day she had caught me off guard. "Biography?" Peter Sinkowitz was coasting down his driveway in a four-wheeled plastic banana; the two little girls were running, screaming after him. "Why would you want to do that?"

She snapped a picture. "Don't you wish somebody came up to you today and gave you a scrapbook called 'The Life of Leo Borlock'? And it's a record, like a journal, of what you did on such-and-such a date when you were little. From the days you can't remember anymore. And there's pictures, and even stuff that you dropped or threw away, like a candy wrapper. And it was all done by some neighbor across the street, and you didn't even know she was doing it. Don't you think when you're fifty or sixty you'd give a fortune to have such a thing?"

I thought about it. It was ten years since I had been six. It seemed like a century. She was right about one thing: I didn't remember much about those days. But I didn't really care either.

"No," I said, "I don't think so. And anyway, don't you think his parents are doing that? Family albums and all?"

One of the little girls managed to wrest the banana roadster away from Peter Sinkowitz. Peter started howling.

"I'm sure they are," she said, snapping another picture. "But those pictures and those moments are posed and smiling. They're not as real as this. Someday he's going to love this picture of himself bawling while a little girl rides off on his toy. I don't follow him around like we did Clarissa. I just keep an eye out for him, and a couple of times a week I jot down what I saw him doing that day. I'll do it for a few more years, then I'll give it to his parents to give to him when he's older and ready to appreciate it." A puzzled look came over her face. She poked me with her elbow. "What?"

"Huh?" I said.

"You're staring at me really funny. What is it?"

I blurted, "Are you running for saint?"

I regretted the words as soon as they left my lips. She just looked at me, hurt in her eyes.

"Sorry," I said. "I didn't mean to sound nasty."

"How did you mean to sound?"

"Amazed, I guess."

"At what?"

I laughed. "What do you think? *You.*" I laughed again. I stood before the steps, facing her. "Look at you. It's Saturday. I've been with you all day, and you've spent the whole day doing stuff for other people. Or paying attention to other people. Or following other people. Or taking pictures of other people."

◀ What is the difference between the pictures Stargirl takes and the pictures parents take of their children, according to Stargirl?

▶ What does Stargirl think Leo is trying to say?

She looked up at me. The hurt was gone from her eyes, but not the puzzlement. She blinked. "So?"

"So . . . I don't know what I'm saying."

"Sounds like you're saying I'm obsessed with other people. Is that it?"

Maybe it was the angle, but her fawn's eyes, looking up at me, seemed larger than ever. I had to make an effort to keep my balance lest I fall into them. "You're different," I said, "that's for sure."

She batted her eyelids and gave me a flirty grin. "Don't you like different?"

"Sure I do," I said, maybe a little too quickly.

A look of sudden discovery brightened her face. She reached out with her foot and tapped my sneaker. "I know what your problem is."

"Really?" I said. "What?"

▶ What does Stargirl think Leo's problem is?

"You're jealous. You're upset because I'm paying all this attention to other people and not enough to you."

"Right," I sniffed. "I'm jealous of Peter Sinkowitz."

She stood. "You just want me all to yourself, don't you?" She stepped into my space. The tips of our noses were touching. "Don't you, Mr. Leo?" Her arms were around my neck.

We were on the sidewalk in front of her house, in full view. "What are you doing?" I said.

"I'm giving you some attention," she cooed. "Don't you want some attention?"

I was losing my battle for balance.

"I don't know," I heard myself say.

"You're really dumb," she whispered in my ear.

"Yeah?"

"Yeah. Why do you think there're eighteen pebbles in my wagon?" And then the last remaining space between our lips was gone and I was falling headlong into her eyes, right there on Palo Verde after dinner. And I can tell you, that was no saint kissing me.

Respond to the Selection

Do you think Leo and Stargirl's relationship will last? Explain your answer.

Investigate, Inquire, and Imagine

Recall: GATHERING FACTS

1a. How does Leo react to the smile Stargirl gives him after Leo thanks her for the card?

2a. What happens to Leo when he tries to become nothing?

3a. Why does Stargirl hate change (i.e. pennies, nickels, dimes, and quarters)? What does she do with it?

Interpret: FINDING MEANING

→ 1b. What does his reaction tell you about his feelings for Stargirl?

→ 2b. How would you expect this experience to affect Leo?

→ 3b. Why does she do this? What does this say about Stargirl's character?

Analyze: TAKING THINGS APART

4a. Stargirl's happy wagon has 17 pebbles in her wagon and three beside it at the end of chapter 22. Go back to chapter 14 and estimate how many pebbles her wagon contained for chapters 14, 15, 16, 17, 18, 19, 20, and 21. Make a graph of your findings, calling the vertical line "pebbles in the wagon" and the horizontal line "chapter in book" (along the vertical line, number it 0 through 20 on each line up; along the horizontal line, write 14 through 22). Write a short description of your graph.

Synthesize: BRINGING THINGS TOGETHER

→ 4b. What happens in Stargirl's life during these chapters that affects her happiness? What kinds of things make Stargirl happy? What kinds of things make her unhappy?

Evaluate: MAKING JUDGMENTS

5a. Señor Saguaro suggests that Leo decide whose affection he values more, Stargirl's or the other students' at MAHS. Once he's made that decision, what he should do will become obvious. Do you think this is good advice? Why, or why not?

Extend: CONNECTING IDEAS

→ 5b. Would you be willing to ask someone you care about to change to make that person more like "other people"? Explain your answer.

Understanding Literature

SUSPENSE. **Suspense** is a feeling of expectation, anxiousness, or curiosity created by questions raised in the mind of the reader or viewer. Identify three ways in which Spinelli creates suspense in Chapters 14–22. Then as you read, track other suspenseful elements.

METAPHOR. A **metaphor** is a figure of speech in which one thing is spoken or written about as if it were another. This figure of speech invites the reader to make a comparison between the two things. Find examples of three metaphors in Chapters 14–22.

DESCRIPTION. A **description** portrays a character, an object, or a scene. Descriptions make use of sensory details—words and phrases that describe how things look, sound, smell, taste, or feel. What details are used to describe the enchanted place?

Chapter 23

Those were the best times, when we were alone, together, out of school. We took long walks around town and into the desert, to her enchanted place. We sat on park benches and people-watched. I introduced her to strawberry-banana smoothies. I borrowed the pickup and drove us to Red Rock and Glendale. On weekends we went to Archie's. On his back porch, we talked of a thousand things and laughed and swooned in pipesmoke and ate pizza. She presented her oratorical contest speech to Señor Saguaro. We never spoke of the shunning. I loved weekends.

But Mondays always followed Sundays.

And the shunning—it was clear now—had come to me. It was less absolute for me than for her, but it was there. I saw it in the eyes that shifted away from mine, the shoulders that turned, the chatter that seemed less loud around me now than before. I fought it. I tested its limits. In the courtyard, between classes, in the lunchroom, I called out to others just to see if they would respond. When someone turned and nodded, I felt grateful. If someone spoke to me, especially if I had not spoken first, I wanted to cry. I had never realized how much I needed the attention of others to confirm my own presence.

◄ What realization does Leo make about himself?

I told myself that the shunning was more painful for me than for Stargirl. I told myself that she was too busy being herself to notice that she was being ignored—and in fact, she continued to give birthday people a ukulele serenade and to decorate her desk and to distribute assorted kindnesses. I told myself that even if she did notice, she wouldn't care.

I understood why this was happening to me. In the eyes of the student body, she was part of my identity. I was "her boyfriend." I was Mr. Stargirl.

Students said things. Not to me, not directly, but tuned for me to overhear even as they pretended I was nowhere near. They said she was a self-centered spotlight hogger. They said she thought she was some kind of saint—I cringed at that—and that she was better than the rest of us. They said she wanted everyone else to feel guilty for not being as nice and wonderful as she was. They said she was a phony.

Most of all, they said she was the reason why the Mica Electrons were not soon to become Arizona state basketball champions. Kevin had been right: when she started cheering for other teams, she did something bad to her own team. To see one of their own priming the opposition did something to the team's morale that hours of practice could not overcome. And the last straw—everyone seemed to agree—was the Sun Valley game, when Stargirl rushed across the court to aid Kovac, the Sun Valley star. All of this was affirmed by our own star, Ardsley himself, who said that when he saw a Mica cheerleader giving comfort to the enemy, the heart went out of him. She was why they lost the next game so miserably to Red Rock. They hated her for it, and they would never forgive.

▶ What is the last straw?

Unlike Stargirl, I was aware of the constant anger of our schoolmates, <u>seething</u> like snakes under a porch. In fact, I was not only aware of it, but at times I also understood their point of view. There were even moments when something small and huddled within me agreed with it. But then I would see her smile and take a swan dive into her eyes, and the bad moment would be gone.

I saw. I heard. I understood. I suffered. But whose sake was I suffering for? I kept thinking of Señor Saguaro's question: *Whose affection do you value more, hers or the others'?*

▶ What does Leo resent?

I became angry. I resented having to choose. I refused to choose. I imagined my life without her and without them, and I didn't like it either way. I pretended it would not always be like this. In the magical moonlight of my bed at night, I pretended she would become more like them and they would become more like her, and in the end I would have it all.

Then she did something that made pretending impossible.

words
for
everyday
use

seethe (sēth′) v., be in a state of rapid agitated movement; suffer violent internal excitement. *The group of students were <u>seething</u> with anger after watching the fight take place.*

Chapter 24

"Roadrunner."

No one said the word to me directly, but I kept hearing it since I arrived at school one day, several days after the kiss on the sidewalk. It seemed more dropped behind than spoken, so that I kept walking into it:

"Roadrunner."

Was there something on the plywood roadrunner that I should read?

I had study hall coming up third period; I'd look into it then. In the meantime, I had second-period Spanish. As I headed for my seat, I looked out the window, which faced the courtyard. There was something written on the roadrunner, all right, but I wouldn't have to go outside to read it. I could read it from here. I could have read it from a low-flying airplane. White paper—no, it was a bedsheet—covered the whole bird. Painted on the sheet in broad red brush strokes was a Valentine heart enclosing the words:

◀ *On what does Stargirl write "Stargirl Loves Leo" that is attached to the roadrunner?*

STARGIRL
LOVES
LEO

My first impulse was to drag the Spanish teacher to the window and say, "Look! She loves me!" My second impulse was to run outside and rip the sign away.

Until now, I had never been the target of her public extravagance. I felt a sudden, strange kinship with Hillari Kimble: I understood why she had commanded Stargirl not to sing to her. I felt spotlighted on a bare stage.

I couldn't concentrate on my schoolwork or anything else. I was a mess.

At lunch that day, I was afraid to look at her. I counted one blessing: I had not yet worked up the nerve to sit with her each day. I kept <u>stoking</u> my conversation with Kevin. I felt her presence, her eyes,

---

words
for
everyday
use

stoke (stōk′) v., stir up or feed fuel to. *The cheerleaders performed one routine after another, trying to <u>stoke</u> the crowd's enthusiasm.*

▶ Who is the only friend who has not deserted Stargirl?

three tables to my left. I knew she was sitting there with Dori Dilson, the only friend who had not deserted her. I felt the faint tug of her gaze on the back of my neck. Ignoring my wishes, my head turned on its own and there she was: smiling to beat the band, waving grandly, and—horrors!—blowing me a kiss. I snapped my head back and dragged Kevin out of the lunchroom.

When I finally dared to look again at the courtyard, I found that someone had torn the sign away. Thumbtacks at the corners pinned four white scraps of bedsheet to the plywood.

I managed to avoid her by taking different routes between classes, but she found me after school, came shouting after me as I tried to slink away: "Leo! Leo!"

She ran up to me, breathless, bursting, her eyes sparkling in the sun. "Did you see it?"

I nodded. I kept walking.

"Well?" She was hopping beside me, punching my shoulder. "Wha'd you think?"

What could I say? I didn't want to hurt her feelings. I just shrugged.

"Wow. That impressed, huh?" She was mocking me. She reached into her bag and pulled out her rat. "Maybe he's shy, Cinnamon. Maybe he'll tell you how thrilled he was to see the sign." She set him on my shoulder.

I yelped. I swept the rat off and sent him flying to the ground.

She scooped him up and stroked him, all the while staring at me dumbstruck. I could not face her. I turned and walked on alone.

She called, "I guess you don't want to hear me practice my speech, huh?"

I did not answer. I did not look back.

The next day I faced the full impact of the sign. I thought I had truly suffered from the spillover of Stargirl's shunning, but that was nothing now that the full <u>torrent</u> was turned on me.

Of course Kevin—thankfully—talked to me; so did a few other friends. But the rest was silence, a second desert imposed upon the one I already lived in, where "Hi" was as rare as rain. I came to the courtyard in the morning before opening bell, and all I saw were backs of heads. People shouldered past me, calling others. Doors closed in my face. There was laughter, there was fun, but it skipped over me like a flat stone on water.

One morning as I was running a teacher's errand, I saw someone named Renshaw walking across the courtyard. I barely knew the kid, but we were the only two in the courtyard at that moment, and I had to, so to speak, touch the stove that I knew was hot. "Renshaw!" I called. There was no other voice but mine. *"Renshaw!"* He never turned, never <u>wavered</u>, never slowed down. He kept walking away from me, opened a door, and was gone.

So what? I kept telling myself. What do you care? You never speak to each other. What's Renshaw to you?

But I did care. I couldn't help myself from caring. At that moment, there was nothing more I wanted in the world than a nod from Renshaw. I prayed that the door would burst open and he would be there saying, "Sorry, Borlock, I wasn't listening. What did you want?" But the door stayed closed, and I knew what it felt like to be invisible.

"I'm invisible," I said to Kevin at lunch. "Nobody hears me. Nobody sees me. I'm the friggin' invisible man."

Kevin just looked at his lunch and wagged his head.

"How long's it going to go on?" I demanded.

He shrugged.

"What did I *do?*" My voice was louder than I intended.

He chewed. He stared. At last he said, "You know what you did."

I stared at him like he was crazy. I badgered him some more. But of course he was perfectly right. I knew exactly what I had done. I had linked myself to an unpopular person. That was my crime.

◀ What does Leo see and hear when he arrives in the courtyard in the morning before opening bell?

◀ What does Leo want more than anything from Renshaw?

words for everyday use

tor • rent (tôr′ ənt) *n.,* swift, violent stream. *Once the rain began to fall in full <u>torrent</u>, not a single car could be seen on the streets.*

wa • ver (wā′ vər) *v.,* sway unsteadily. *Although I did see her <u>waver</u> once, Becky performed a strong balance beam routine.*

Chapter 25

Days passed. I continued to avoid Stargirl. I wanted her. I wanted them. It seemed I could not have both, so I did nothing. I ran and hid.

But she did not give up on me. She hunted me down. She found me in the TV studio after school one day. I felt fingers slipping down the back of my neck, grabbing my collar, pulling me backward. The crew was staring. "Mr. Borlock," I heard her say, "we need to talk." Her voice told me she was not smiling. She released my collar. I followed her out of the room.

In the courtyard a couple cooing on the bench beneath the palmetto[1] saw us coming and bolted, so that's where we sat.

"So," she said, "are we breaking up already?"

"I don't want to," I said.

"So why are you hiding from me?"

Forced to face her, forced to talk, I felt my <u>gumption</u> rising. "Something's gotta change," I said. "That's all I know."

"You mean like change clothes? Or change a tire? Should I change a tire on my bike? Would that do it?"

"You're not funny. You know what I mean."

She saw I was upset. Her face got serious.

"People aren't talking to me," I said. I stared at her. I wanted it to sink in. "People I've known ever since we moved here. They don't talk to me. They don't *see* me."

She reached out and lightly rubbed the back of my hand with her fingertip. Her eyes were sad. "I'm sorry people don't see you. It's no fun not being seen, is it?"

I pulled my hand away. "Well, you tell me what it's like. Doesn't it bother you that nobody talks to you?" It was the first time I had openly mentioned the shunning to her.

▶ *What is Leo's response to Stargirl when she asks why he's hiding from her?*

---

1. **palmetto**. Low-growing, fan-leafed palms

words for everyday use   gump • tion (gəm(p)' shən) *n.*, shrewd common sense, courage, and initiative. *The mother's* <u>gumption</u> *helped her put an end to the chaotic scene.*

She smiled. "Dori talks to me. You talk to me. Archie talks to me. My family talks to me. Cinnamon talks to me. Señor Saguaro talks to me. *I* talk to me." She cocked her head and stared at me, waiting for a responding smile. I didn't give it. "Are *you* going to stop talking to me?"

"That's not the question," I said.

"What *is* the question?"

"The question is"—I tried to read her face but I could not—"what makes you tick?"

"Now I'm a *clock!*"

I turned away. "See, I can't talk to you. It's all just a big joke."

She put my face between her hands and turned me to her. I hoped people were not watching from the windows. "Okay, serious now. Go ahead, ask me the tick question again. Or any other, any question at all."

I shook my head. "You just don't care, do you?"

That stumped her. "Care? Leo, how can you say I don't care? You've gone with me to places. We've delivered cards and flowers. How can you say—"

"That's not what I mean. I mean you don't care what people think."

"I care what *you* think. I care—"

"I know—you care what Cinnamon and Señor Saguaro think. I'm talking about the school, the town. I'm talking about everybody."

She sniffed around the word. "Everybody?"

"Right. You don't seem to care what everybody thinks. You don't seem to *know* what everybody thinks. You—"

She broke in: "Do you?"

I thought for a moment. I nodded sharply. "Yeah. Yeah, I think I do know. I'm in touch with everybody. I'm one of them. How could I not know?"

"And it matters?"

"Sure, it matters. Look"—I waved my arm at the school around us—"look what's happening. Nobody talks to us. You can't just not give a crap what anybody thinks. You can't just cheer for the other team and expect your own school to love you for it." Words that I had been thinking for weeks rolled off

◀ *Does it bother Stargirl that nobody is talking to her?*

my tongue now. "Kovac—Kovac, for God's sake. What was *that* all about?"

She was baffled. "Who's Kovac?"

"Kovac. The guy from Sun Valley. The basketball star. The guy who broke his ankle."

She was still baffled. "What about him?"

"What about him? What about *you*? What were you doing out there on the floor with him with his head in your lap?"

"He was in pain."

"He was the *enemy,* Stargirl! Susan. Whatever. The *enemy!*" She stared dumbly back at me. She had blinked at "Susan." "There were a thousand Sun Valley people there. He had his *own* people to take care of him, his *own* coaches, his *own* teammates, his *own* cheerleaders' laps. And you had *your* own team to worry about." I was screeching. I got up and walked away. I came back, leaned into her. "Why," I said. "Why didn't you just let him be taken care of by his own people?"

She looked at me for a long time, as if in my face she could find herself explained. "I don't know," she said dimly at last. "I didn't think. I just did."

I pulled back. I was tempted to say, *Well, I hope you're satisfied, because they hate you for what you did,* but I didn't have the heart.

Now I was feeling sorry for her. I sat back down beside her. I took her hand. I smiled. I spoke as gently as I could. "Stargirl, you just can't do things the way you do. If you weren't stuck in a homeschool all your life, you'd understand. You can't just wake up in the morning and say you don't care what the rest of the world thinks."

Her eyes were wide, her voice peepy like a little girl's. "You can't?"

"Not unless you want to be a hermit."

She flicked the hem of her skirt at my sneaker, dusting it. "But how do you keep track of the rest of the world? Sometimes I can hardly keep track of myself."

"It's not something you even have to think about," I said. "You just know. Because you're connected."

▶ Why did Stargirl go to Kovac and hold his head in her lap?

▶ Why didn't Stargirl let Kovac be taken care of by his teammates?

On the ground her bag shifted slightly: Cinnamon was stirring. Stargirl's face went through a series of expressions, ending with a pout and a sudden sobby outburst: "I'm not connected!" She reached out to me and we hugged on the bench in the courtyard and walked home together.

We continued this conversation for the next couple of days. I explained the ways of people to her. I said you can't cheer for everybody. She said why not? I said a person belongs to a group, you can't belong to everyone. She said why not? I said you can't just barge into the funeral of a perfect stranger. She said why not? I said you just can't. She said why? I said because. I said you have to respect other people's privacy, there's such a thing as not being welcome. I said not everybody likes having somebody with a ukulele sing "Happy Birthday" to them. They don't? she said.

◀ What does Leo say about belonging?

This group thing, I said, it's very strong. It's probably an instinct. You find it everywhere, from little groups like families to big ones like a town or school, to really big ones like a whole country. How about really, *really* big ones, she said, like a planet? Whatever, I said. The point is, in a group everybody acts pretty much the same, that's kind of how the group holds itself together. Everybody? she said. Well, mostly, I said. That's what jails and mental hospitals are for, to keep it that way. You think I should be in jail? she said. I think you should try to be more like the rest of us, I said.

Why? she said.

Because, I said.

Tell me, she said.

It's hard, I said.

Say it, she said.

Because nobody likes you, I said. That's why. Nobody likes you.

Nobody? she said. Her eyes covered me like the sky. *Nobody?*

I tried to play dumb, but that wasn't working. Hey, I said, don't look at me. We're talking about them. *Them.* If it was up to me, I wouldn't change a thing.

You're fine with me the way you are. But we're not alone, are we? We live in a world of them, like it or not.

▶ What does Leo not say?

That's where I tried to keep it, on them. I didn't mention myself. I didn't say do it for me. I didn't say if you don't change you can forget about me. I never said that.

Two days later Stargirl vanished.

Chapter 26

Usually I saw her in the courtyard before school, but that day I didn't. Usually I passed her between classes at least once or twice before lunch. Not that day. In fact, when I looked over to her table at lunch, there was Dori Dilson, as usual, but someone else was sitting with her. No Stargirl in sight.

Coming out of the lunchroom, I heard laughter behind me. And then a voice, Stargirl's: "What do you have to do to get somebody's attention around here?"

I turned, but it wasn't her. The girl standing, grinning in front of me wore jeans and sandals, had burnt-red nails and lipstick, painted eyes, finger rings, toe rings, hoop earrings I could put my hand through, hair . . .

◀ What is the girl standing in front of Leo wearing?

I gawked as students swarmed past. She made a clownish grin. She was beginning to look vaguely familiar. Tentatively I whispered, "Stargirl?"

She batted her chocolaty eyelashes. "Stargirl? What kind of name is that? My name is Susan."

And just like that, Stargirl was gone, replaced by Susan. Susan Julia Caraway. The girl she might have been all along.

I couldn't take my eyes off her. She cradled her books in her arms. The sunflower canvas bag was gone. The rat was gone. The ukulele was gone. She turned around slowly for my open-mouthed, dumbstruck inspection. Nothing goofy, nothing different could I see. She looked magnificently, wonderfully, gloriously ordinary. She looked just like a hundred other girls at Mica High. Stargirl had vanished into a sea of *them,* and I was thrilled. She slid a stick of chewing gum into her mouth and chewed away noisily. She winked at me. She reached out and tweaked my cheek the way my grandmother would and said, "What's up, cutie?" I grabbed her, right there outside the lunchroom in the swarming mob. I didn't care if

---

words for everyday use ten • ta • tive (tən' tə tiv) *adj.,* hesitant; uncertain. *I took a small, tentative step into the darkness, worried I was going to knock something over.*

others were watching. In fact, I hoped they were. I grabbed her and squeezed her. I had never been so happy and so proud in my life.

We sailed through time. We held hands in the hallways, on the stairs, in the courtyard. In the lunchroom I grabbed her and pulled her over to our table. I looked to invite Dori Dilson, too, but she was gone. I sat there grinning while Kevin and Susan gabbed and gossiped over their sandwiches. They joked about her disastrous appearance on *Hot Seat.* Susan suggested that I should go on *Hot Seat* one of these days, and Kevin said no, he's too shy, and I said not anymore, and we all laughed.

▶ *Why doesn't Leo invite Dori Dilson?*

And it was true. I didn't walk, I strutted. I was Susan Caraway's boyfriend. I. Me. Really? *That* Susan Caraway? The one with the tiny barrettes and toe rings? Yep, that's the one, my girlfriend. Call me Mr. Susan.

I started saying "we" instead of "I," as in "We'll meet you there" or "We like fajitas."

Whenever I could, I said her name out loud, like blowing bubbles. The rest of the time I said it to myself.

Susan . . . Susan . . .

We did our homework together. We hung out with Kevin. Instead of following strangers around, we went to the movies and plunged our hands together into the six-dollar Super Tub of popcorn. Instead of shopping for African violets, we shopped for Cinnabons and licked icing from each other's fingers.

We went into Pisa Pizza. We walked past the bulletin board inside the door. We shared a pizza: half pepperoni, half anchovies.

"Anchovies, ugh," I said.

"What's wrong with anchovies?" she said.

"How can you eat them? Nobody eats anchovies."

I was sort of kidding, but her face was serious. "Nobody?"

"Nobody I know."

▶ *What does Susan do to her anchovies?*

She picked the anchovies from her slices and dumped them into her water glass.

I tried to stop her. "Hey—"

She pushed my hand away. She dropped the last anchovy into the glass. "I don't want to be like nobody."

On the way out, we ignored the bulletin board.

She was mad for shopping. It was as if she had just discovered clothes. She bought shirts and pants and shorts and costume jewelry and makeup. I began to notice that the items of clothing had one thing in common: they all had the designer's name plastered <u>prominently</u> on them. She seemed to buy not for color or style but for designer label size.

She constantly quizzed me about what other kids would do, would buy, would say, would think. She invented a fictitious person whom she called Evelyn Everybody. "Would Evelyn like this?" "Would Evelyn do that?"

Sometimes she misfired, as with laughing. For several days she was on a laughing jag. She didn't just laugh, she boomed. Heads turned in the lunchroom. I was trying to work up the nerve to say something when she looked at Kevin and me and said, "Would Evelyn laugh this much?" Kevin stared at his sandwich. I sheepishly shook my head. The laughing stopped, and from that moment on she did a perfect imitation of a sullen, pout-lipped teenager.

◀ *How does Susan laugh?*

In every way she seemed to be a typical, ordinary, everyday, run-of-the-mill teenager.

And it wasn't working.

At first I neither noticed nor much cared that the shunning continued. I was too busy being happy that she was, as I saw it, now one of us. My only regret was that we could not play the basketball season over again. In my mind's eye, I pictured her aiming her incredible <u>zeal</u> and energy exclusively at the Electrons. We could have won games on her cheering alone.

It was she who said it first: "They still don't like me." We were standing outside the TV studio after school.

words for everyday use prom • i • nent (prä' mə nənt) *adj.,* standing out, conspicuous. *The <u>prominent</u> placement of the ad was sure to draw in customers.* **prominently,** *adv.*

zeal (zēal) *n.,* eagerness, enthusiasm. *Her <u>zeal</u> for cooking left her whipping up large amounts of delicious food.*

As usual, people were passing by as if we weren't there. Her lip quivered. "What am I doing wrong?" Tears made her eyes even larger.

I squeezed her hand. I told her to give it some time. I pointed out that the state basketball finals would take place in Phoenix that Saturday, and that would end the season and clear the way for her cheerleading crimes to be forgotten.

Her mascara was muddy. I had seen her sad many times before, but always for someone else. This was different. This was for herself, and I was powerless to help. I could not find it in me to cheer up the cheerleader.

That night we did homework together at her house. I ducked into her room to check out her happy wagon. There were only two stones in it.

▶ How many stones are in Susan's happy wagon?

When I came to school next day, there was something different about the buzz in the courtyard. The arriving students were milling about, some roaming at random, some in clusters, but as I approached, there seemed to be a distinct clearing around the palmetto. I wandered in that direction, and through the crowd I could see that someone—Susan—was seated on the bench. She sat upright and smiling. She was holding a foot-long stick shaped like a claw on one end. Around her neck, dangling on a string, was a sign that read: TALK TO ME AND I'LL SCRATCH YOUR BACK. She was getting no takers. No one was within twenty feet of her.

Quickly I turned away. I walked back through the crowd. I pretended I was looking for someone. I pretended I hadn't seen. And prayed for the bell to ring.

When I saw her later that morning, the sign was gone. She said nothing about it. Neither did I.

Next morning she came running at me in the courtyard. Her eyes were bright for the first time in days. She grabbed me with both hands and shook me. "It's going to be okay! It's going to end! I had a vision!"

She told me about it. She had gone to her enchanted place after dinner the day before, and that's where the vision had come to her. She had seen herself returning in triumph from the Arizona state oratorical contest. She had won first prize. Best in the state. When she returned, she got a hero's welcome. The whole school greeted her in the parking lot, just like in the assembly film. There were streamers and confetti and tooting kazoos[1] and horns blaring, and the mayor and city council were on hand, and they had a parade right then and there, and she rode high on the back seat of a convertible and held her winner's silver plate up for all to see, and the happy faces of her classmates flashed in the sparkling trophy. She told me this, and she threw up her arms and shouted, "I'm going to be popular!"

The state contest was a week away. Every day she practiced her speech. One day she called over little Peter Sinkowitz and his playmates and presented the speech to us from her front steps. We applauded and whistled. She bowed grandly, and I, too, began to see her vision. I saw the streamers flying and I heard the crowd cheering, and I believed.

◀ What happened in Susan's vision after she won the state oratorical contest?

---

1. **kazoos.** Instruments that add a buzzing quality to the human voice and that usually consist of a small metal or plastic tube with a top hole covered by a thin membrane

Chapter 27

". . . and our best wishes go with you, Susan Caraway."

The PA announcement echoed through the school lobby, and we were off to Phoenix. The driver was Mr. McShane, Mica High's faculty representative to the state contest. Susan and I sat in the back. Susan's parents were driving their own car and would meet us in Phoenix.

▶ Who is Mr. McShane?

As we pulled out of the parking lot, she wagged a finger in my face. "Don't get a big head, mister. I was allowed to invite two friends along. You weren't the only one I asked."

"So who was the other?" I said.

"Dori."

"Well, then," I said, "I think I'll go for the big head. Dori isn't another guy."

She grinned. "No, she's not one of those." Suddenly she unbuckled her seat belt—we each had a back window. "Mr. McShane," she announced, "I'm moving over so I can sit close to Leo. He's so cute, I can't help myself."

In the rearview mirror, the teacher's eyes crinkled. "Whatever you like, Susan. It's your day."

She slid over and fastened herself into the middle belt. She jabbed me. "Hear that? It's my day. I get whatever I want."

"So," I said, "what happened when you asked Dori Dilson?"

"She said no. She's mad at me."

"I could tell."

"Ever since I became Susan. She thinks I betrayed myself. She just doesn't understand how important it is to be popular."

I wasn't sure what to say to that. I was feeling a little uneasy. Fortunately, wondering what to say wasn't much of a problem for me during that two-hour ride, because Susan chattered away like the old Stargirl the whole time.

"But I know Dori," she said, "and I'll tell you one thing."

"What's that?"

"She'll be in the front of the mob cheering for me when we get back tomorrow."

I later found out that after we left the school, the principal had spoken again on the PA. He announced our expected time of return on Saturday and suggested that everyone be on hand to meet us, win or lose.

Losing, as it turned out, never occurred to the contestant herself.

"Would you do a favor for me?" she said.

I told her sure.

"That big silver plate that goes to the winner? I'm such a klutz with dishes at home. Would you hold it for me when the crowd rushes us? I'm afraid I'll drop it."

I stared at her. "What crowd? What rush?"

"In the school parking lot. When we get back tomorrow. There's always a crowd waiting for the returning hero. Remember the film at school? My vision?" She cocked her head and peered into my eyes. She rapped my forehead with her knuckle. "Hello in there. Anybody home?"

"Oh," I said. "*That* crowd."

She nodded. "Exactly. Of course, we'll be safe as long as we're in the car. But once we get out, who knows what will happen. Crowds can get pretty wild. Right, Mr. McShane?"

The teacher nodded. "So I hear."

She spoke to me as if instructing a first-grader. "Leo, this has never happened in Mica before, having a winner of the Arizona state oratorical contest. One of their very own. When they hear about it, they're going to go bananas. And when they get a gander at me and that trophy—" She rolled her eyes and whistled. "I just hope they don't get out of hand."

"The police will keep them in line," I said. "Maybe they'll call out the National Guard."

She stared wide-eyed. "You think?" She didn't realize I was kidding. "Well," she said, "I'm really not

◀ What favor does Susan want Leo to do for her?

words
for
everyday
use

gan • der (gan′ dər) n., look, glance. *He took a gander outside to see if he could spot his ride.*

afraid for myself. I won't mind a little jostling. Do you think they'll jostle, Mr. McShane?"

In the mirror his eyes shifted to us. "Never can tell."

"And if they want to carry me around on their shoulders, that's okay, too. But they better not"—she poked me with her finger—"better *not* mess with my trophy. That's why *you*"—another poke—"are going to hold it. Tight."

▶ How does Susan plan to protect her trophy from the mob?

I wished Mr. McShane would say something. "Susan," I said, "did you ever hear of counting your chickens?"

"Before they hatch, you mean?"

"Exactly."

"I hear you're not supposed to."

"Exactly."

She nodded thoughtfully. "Never made much sense to me. I mean, if you *know* they're going to hatch, why not count them?"

"Because you can't know," I said. "There's no guarantees. I hate to break this to you, but you're not the only person in the contest. Somebody else *could* win. You *could* lose. It's possible."

She thought about that for a moment, then shook her head. "Nope. Not possible. So . . ." She threw up her arms and smiled hugely. "Why wait to feel great? Celebrate now, that's my motto." She nuzzled into me. "What's yours, big boy?"

"Don't count your chickens," I said.

She shuddered mockingly. "Ouuu. You're such a poop, Leo. What's your motto, Mr. McShane?"

▶ What is Mr. McShane's motto?

"Drive carefully," he said, "you may have a winner in the car."

That set her off howling.

"Mr. McShane," I said, "you're not helping."

"Sorry," he lied.

I just looked at her. "You're going to be in a state contest," I said. "Aren't you just a little bit nervous?"

The smile vanished. "Yes, I am. I'm a lot nervous. I just hope things don't get out of hand when we get back to the school. I've never been adored by mobs of people before. I'm not sure how I'm going to react. I hope I don't get a big head. Do you think I'm the big-head type, Mr. McShane?"

I raised my hand. "Can I answer that?"

"I think your head is just fine," said the teacher.

She jabbed me with her elbow. "Hear that, Mr. Know-it-all?" She gave me her smug face, which promptly disappeared as she thrust up her arms and yelped, "They're going to love me!"

Mr. McShane wagged his head and chuckled. Silently I gave up.

She pointed out the window. "Look, even the desert is celebrating."

It seemed to be true. The normally dull cacti and scrub were splashed with April colors, as if a great painter had passed over the landscape with a brush, dabbing yellow here, red there.

Susan strained against her seat belt. "Mr. McShane, can we stop here, just for a minute? Please?" When the teacher hesitated, she added, "You said it's my day. I get whatever I want."

◀ What does Susan ask Mr. McShane to do as they pass the desert landscape?

The car coasted to a stop along the gravelly road-side. In a moment, she was out the door and bounding across the desert. She skipped and whirled and cartwheeled among the prickly natives. She bowed to a yucca, waltzed with a saguaro. She plucked a red blossom from a barrel cactus and fixed it in her hair. She practiced her smile and her nod and her wave—one-hand, two-hand—to the adoring mob at her hero's welcome. She snapped a needle from a cactus and with the slapstick pantomime of a circus clown pretended to pick her teeth with it.

Mr. McShane and I were leaning on the car, laughing, when suddenly she stopped, cocked her head, and stared off in another direction. She stayed like that, stone still, for a good two minutes, then abruptly turned and came back to the car.

Her face was thoughtful. "Mr. McShane," she said as the teacher drove off, "do you know any extinct birds?"

"Passenger pigeon," he said. "That's probably the best known. They say there used to be so many of

---

words for everyday use

abrupt (ə brəpt') adj., without preparation or warning; unexpected. *The clerk's abrupt departure left the store understaffed.* abruptly, adv.

How tall did the moa grow?

them they would darken the sky when they flew over. And the moa."

"Moa?"

"Huge bird."

"Like a condor?" I said.

He chuckled. "A condor wouldn't come up to its knee. Make an ostrich look small. Twelve, thirteen feet tall. Maybe the biggest bird ever. Couldn't fly. Lived in New Zealand. Died out hundreds of years ago. Killed off by people."

"Half their size," said Susan.

Mr. McShane nodded. "Mm. I wrote a report about moas in grade school. I thought they were the neatest thing."

Susan's eyes were glistening. "Did moas have a voice?"

The teacher thought about it. "I don't know. I don't know if anybody knows."

Susan looked out the window at the passing desert. "I heard a mockingbird back there. And it made me think of something Archie said."

"Mr. Brubaker?" said Mr. McShane.

"Yes. He said he believes mockingbirds may do more than imitate other birds. I mean, other *living* birds. He thinks they may also imitate the sounds of birds that are no longer around. He thinks the sounds of extinct birds are passed down the years from mockingbird to mockingbird."

"Interesting thought," said Mr. McShane.

"He says when a mockingbird sings, for all we know it's pitching fossils into the air. He says who knows what songs of ancient creatures we may be hearing out there."

The words of Archie Brubaker settled over the silence in the car. As if reading my thoughts, Mr. McShane turned off the air conditioner and powered down the windows. Hair blew in a faint, smoky scent of mesquite.

After a while I felt the touch of Susan's hand. Her fingers wove through mine.

"Mr. McShane," she cooed, "we're holding hands in the back seat."

"Uh-oh," he said, "hormonal teenagers."

"Don't you think he's cute, Mr. McShane?"

"I never really thought about it," said the teacher.

"Well, look," she said. She grabbed my face in her hand and pulled it forward. The teacher's eyes considered me briefly in the rearview mirror.

"You're right. He's adorable."

Susan released my blushing face. "Told you. Don't you just love him?"

"I wouldn't go that far."

A minute later: "Mr. McSha-ane . . ." Now I felt something in my ear. "I'm putting my finger in his ear . . ."

This sort of silliness went on until we rounded a mesa and saw the brown mist on the horizon that announced our approach to the city of Phoenix.

◀ What announced their approach to Phoenix?

Chapter 28

Her parents met us in the lobby of the hotel where Susan, Mr. McShane, and I each had a room for the night. After we checked in, the five of us ate a buffet lunch in the hotel restaurant. Then we watched Susan board a bus that would take her and eighteen other contestants to Phoenix West High School. There were thirty-eight contestants; nineteen had already given their speeches that morning.

By the end of the afternoon, ten finalists would be chosen. The finals would take place that evening.

▶ What was the surprise with Susan's speech?

To be honest, none of us was surprised that Susan made the cut. She was incredibly good. The surprise was this: her speech was new. It was not the one she had given at Mica High. It was not the one she had been practicing for weeks in front of me and Peter Sinkowitz and assorted saguaros. It was not the one I had heard just the day before.

But it was wonderful.

There were some elements of the old speech in it, and much that was as new as that morning. Like a butterfly, her words fluttered from image to image. She swung from the distant past (Barney, Archie's Paleocene rodent skull) to the present (Cinnamon) to the distant future (the death of the sun). From the most ordinary here (the old man nodding off on the bench at Tudor Village) to the most extraordinary there (a newly discovered galaxy ninety percent to the end of the universe). She touched on silver lunch trucks and designer labels and enchanted places, and when she said her best friend gave her pet rat a ride on his shoulder, tears came to my eyes. It was a jumble, it was a mishmash, and somehow she pulled it all together, somehow she threaded every different thing through the voice of a solitary mockingbird singing in the desert. She called her speech "I Might Have Heard a Moa."

▶ What does Susan call her speech?

The auditorium was half full, mostly with small groups of students and parents from the competing schools. After a contestant finished, his or her supporters whistled and whooped, as if doing so would influence the judges. The rest was polite applause.

When Susan finished, the four of us managed a modest cheer, but that was about it. No whistles, no whoops. I think we were made of more timid stuff than the speechmaker herself.

Back at the hotel Mr. McShane and I mobbed her, if two can be a mob. Her parents were more reserved. They were full of smiles and "well dones," but they seemed no more surprised at her success than Susan did.

When the adults went off to the gift shop, I had her to myself. I said, "Where did *that* come from?"

She grinned. "Did you like it?"

"Sure, but it's not what I've been hearing for the last month. What were you doing, practicing a secret speech on the side?"

The grin got wider. "Nope. That was the first time I heard it, too."

I stared at her. Slowly her words sank in. "Let me get this straight. You're saying you just made it up this morning?"

"I'm saying I didn't even make it up. It was just there. All I did was open my mouth, and let it out." She held both hands out to me and snapped her fingers. "Presto!"

I gaped at her. "What are you going to say tonight?"

She threw out her arms: "Who knows?"

◀ *What does Susan plan to say tonight?*

The five of us ate an early dinner in the hotel restaurant. Afterward, we waited in the lobby while Susan changed clothes. She stepped off the elevator wearing a peach-colored pantsuit. She slinked across the lobby, modeling for us. She sat on her mother's lap and said, "My personal seamstress made it for me." We applauded lightly and sent her off on the bus.

The general public was invited to the evening show, and the auditorium was packed. People stood in back. Down front, a high school orchestra played rousing music by John Philip Sousa. The ten contestants sat onstage. Seven were boys. All of the

◀ *How do the other contestants appear?*

contestants appeared to be <u>grim</u> and nervous, stiff as manikins, except for Susan, who was bending the ear of the boy sitting next to her. He nodded occasionally but kept his eyes and spine at attention and obviously wished that she would shut up. Susan's parents chuckled knowingly at her behavior, while I tried to disguise a stab of jealousy.

One by one the contestants took the long walk to center stage to give their speeches. The applause was equally hearty for all. A grade school girl in a frilly white dress handed each contestant a bouquet of roses, yellow for the girls, red for the boys. While the girls cradled their roses, the boys looked at them as if they were hand grenades.

Susan was next to last to speak. When her name was called, she bounced up from her chair and practically ran to the microphone. She did a <u>sprightly</u> pirouette, a curtsy, waved her hand in a window-washer motion, and said, "Hi." Accustomed to seeing stiff, mortified contestants, the audience responded with uncertain titters. They didn't know what to make of this unconventional teenager any more than we had on the first day of school. Several bold souls said "Hi" and waved back.

She did not begin, at least not in the usual sense. There was no ringing <u>preamble</u>. She merely stood there comfortably chatting away as if we were all on rocking chairs on her front porch. Murmur drifted toward the ceiling; people were waiting for her to get started. The murmur subsided as it occurred to them that this was it and they were missing it. The quiet that then fell over the auditorium was absolute. I was more tuned in to the audience than to the speaker, and if for the last five minutes of her talk anyone was breathing, I could not detect it. When she finished with barely a whisper—"Can you hear it?"—and leaned with her cupped hand to her ear, fifteen hun-

▶ What can Leo not detect during the last five minutes of Susan's speech?

dred people seemed to inch forward, straining to hear. There were ten seconds of purest stillness. Then she turned abruptly and went back to her chair. Still there was no reaction. What's going on? I wondered. She sat forward in her chair, her hands folded <u>primly</u> in her lap. And then it came, suddenly, explosively, as if everyone had awakened at once. We were all on our feet, clapping and shouting and whistling. I found myself sobbing. The cheering was as wild as that of the crowd at a championship basketball game.

---

words for everyday use prim (prim') *adj.*, stiffly formal and proper. *In the country club, all the women appeared* *prim*—*except for Hannah, who was slouched in her chair wearing jeans and a faded t-shirt.* primly, *adv.*

Chapter 29

She won. As she had said she would.

The silver plate they gave her twinkled like a starburst in a galaxy of flashing cameras. Two TV crews washed her in lights and interviewed her backstage. Strangers mobbed her, citizens of Phoenix gushing, telling her they had been coming to the contest for years and had never heard anything like it. Schoolchildren thrust programs in her face for autographs. Every parent wanted her for a daughter, every teacher for a student.

She was so happy, she was so proud. She yelped and cried when she saw us. She hugged each of us in turn, and I thought she would squeeze the breath out of me.

Back at the hotel everyone already seemed to know: the doorman, the desk manager, the people in the lobby and elevator. Suddenly she had this magical, wonderful power; whoever laid eyes on her smiled. And the English language dwindled to a single word, repeated over and over: "Congratulations!"

▶ What single word is repeated over and over throughout the evening?

We walked—we floated—around the block to burn off our excess energy. Back at the hotel we were invited into the nightclub, even though Susan and I were underage. We drank ginger ales and ordered jalapeño poppers[1] and we all danced to a country and western band while Susan's face beamed on the late news from the TV above the bar. The dance floor was the only place where she did not carry her silver plate.

First thing next morning there she was, sliding under the door of my hotel room: her picture on the front page of the *Arizona Republic*. I sat on the edge of the bed and stared at it, pride welling in me. I read the story. It called her speech "mesmerizing, hypnotic, mysteriously touching." I pictured folded morning papers tossed from cars, landing in driveways all over Mica.

We all met for the breakfast buffet. People stared and nodded and smiled and silently lip-said

---

1. **jalapeño poppers**. Appetizer made with Mexican hot peppers and cream cheese

"Congratulations" across the restaurant. We headed for home in a two-car caravan.

For a while, Susan was her usual chatty self. She put the silver plate on the front seat beside Mr. McShane. She told him it would ride next to him for ten whole minutes, and he could touch it all he wanted. This was his reward, she said, for telling her about moas. As soon as the ten minutes was up, she took back the plate.

◀ What is Mr. McShane's reward for telling Susan about moas?

As we drew nearer to town, the chatter subsided and finally stopped. We rode the last miles in silence. She took my hand. The nearer we came the harder she squeezed. When we hit the outskirts of town, she turned to me and said, "Do I look okay?"

I told her she looked great.

She didn't seem to believe me. She held up the silver plate and studied her reflection.

She turned to me again and looked at me for some time before she spoke. "I've been thinking. This is how I'm going to do it. I'm going to hold on to the plate myself—okay?"

I nodded.

". . . until . . . until they lift me onto their shoulders. Then I give it to you. Understand?"

I nodded.

"So stay next to me. Every second. Crowds can separate you, you know. They do that. Okay?"

◀ What does Susan say about crowds?

I nodded. "Okay."

Her hand was hot and sweating.

We drove past a man in his driveway. He was dipping a large, broomlike brush into a pail and painting the asphalt with black sealer. He was bent intently to his work in the noonday sun, and somehow I knew at that moment what would happen, I could see it. I wanted to shout to Mr. McShane, "No, don't turn! Don't go there!"

But he did turn. He turned, and there was the school in front of us, and never in my life have I seen a place so empty. No banners, no people, no cars.

"Probably around back," Mr. McShane said. His voice was hoarse. "Parking lot."

We swung around back to the parking lot and—yes—there was a car, and another car. And people,

▶ Who is waiting at the school to greet Susan?

three of them, shading their eyes in the sun, watching us. Two of them were teachers. The other was a student, Dori Dilson. She stood apart from the teachers, alone in the black shimmering sea of asphalt. As we approached, she held up a sign, a huge cardboard sign bigger than a basketball backboard. She set the sign on edge and propped it up, erasing herself. The red painted letters said:

WAY TO GO,
SUSAN
WE'RE PROUD OF
YOU

The car stopped in front of it. All that was left to see of Dori Dilson were two sets of fingers holding the sides of the sign. We were close enough now to see that the sign was trembling, and I knew that behind it Dori was crying. There was no confetti, no kazoos. Nothing cheered, not even a mockingbird.

Chapter 30

As we idled, stunned and silent in front of Dori Dilson's sign, Susan's parents came and retrieved her from Mr. McShane's car. As in all things, they did not appear especially surprised or emotional over what was happening. Susan seemed in a trance. She sat beside me, staring <u>vacantly</u> at the sign through the windshield. Her hand was no longer holding mine. I groped for words but could not find them. When her parents came, she allowed herself to be led away. As she got out of the car, the silver plate slid from her lap and rang like a dying bell against the asphalt. Her father picked it up. I thought he would take it, but instead he leaned into the back seat where I sat and with a strange smile gave it to me.

◀ How do Susan's parents react to the lack of crowd waiting for her?

I did not see her for the rest of the weekend. By Monday she was Stargirl again. Floor-length skirt. Ribbons in her hair. Just like that.

She went from table to table at lunchtime, passing out happy-face cookies. She even gave one to Hillari Kimble. Hillari took off her shoe and used it like a hammer to smash the cookie on her table. Stargirl strolled among us strumming her ukulele, asking for requests. Cinnamon perched on her shoulder. He was strapped onto a tiny toy ukulele. She made her voice squeaky and kept her lips from moving and it was as if Cinnamon were serenading with her. Dori Dilson, bless her, stood and applauded. She was the only one. I was too stunned to join her. And too cowardly. And angry. And not wanting to show approval for her return to Stargirl. Most of the students did not even look, did not even seem to listen. At the bell, as we left the lunchroom, I looked back. The tables were littered with cookies.

Walking with her after school that day, I said, "I guess you're giving up, huh?"

She looked at me. "Giving up? On what?"

---

words for everyday use va • cant (vā′ kənt) *adj.*, devoid of thought, reflection, or expression. *When I saw the* <u>vacant</u> *look in Spencer's eyes, I knew he had not heard a word I'd said.* **vacantly,** *adv.*

"On being popular. On being . . ." How could I say it?

She smiled. "Normal?"

I shrugged.

"Yes," she said firmly.

"Yes?"

▶ What is Stargirl giving up on?

"I'm answering your question. The answer is yes. I'm giving up on trying to be popular and normal." Her face and body language did not seem to match her words. She looked cheery, perky. So did Cinnamon, perched on her shoulder.

"Don't you think maybe you should back off a little?" I said. "Don't come on so strong?"

She smiled at me. She reached out and brushed the tip of my nose with her fingertip. "Because we live in a world of *them*, right? You told me that once."

We stared at each other. She kissed me on the cheek and walked away. She turned and said, "I know you're not going to ask me to the Ocotillo Ball. It's okay." She gave me her smile of infinite kindness and understanding, the smile I had seen her aim at so many other needy souls, and in that moment I hated her.

That very night, as if he were playing a scripted role, Kevin called me and said, "So, who are you taking to the Ocotillo Ball?"

I dodged. "Who are *you* taking?"

"Don't know," he said.

"I don't either."

There was a pause on the other end of the line. "Not Stargirl?"

"Not necessarily," I said.

"You trying to tell me something?"

"What would I want to tell you?"

"I thought you were a two. I thought there was no question."

"So why are you asking?" I said, and hung up.

In bed that night, I became more and more uncomfortable as the moonlight crept up my sheet. I did something I had never done before. I pulled down the shade. In my dreams the old man on the mall bench raised a wobbling head and croaked, "How dare you forgive me."

Next morning there was a new item on the plywood roadrunner, a sheet of white paper. At the top it said:

Sign Up Here to Join
New Musical Group,
THE UKEE DOOKS
No Experience Necessary

There were two numbered columns for names, forty in all. By the end of the day all forty were filled in, with names such as Minnie Mouse and Darth Vader and The Swamp Thing. The principal's name was there, too. And Wayne Parr. And Dori Dilson.

◀ How many people could sign up to join The Ukee Dooks?

"Did you see?" said Kevin. "Somebody wrote in Parr's name."

We were in the studio control room. It was May and our *Hot Seats* were over for the year, but on some days we still <u>gravitated</u> to the studio after school.

"I saw," I said.

He stepped up to a blank monitor, studied his reflection. "So, I didn't see your name on the list."

"Nope."

"You don't want to be a Ukee Dook?"

"Guess not."

We fiddled with the equipment for a while. Kevin walked out onto the stage. He flipped a switch. His mouth moved, but I couldn't hear. I held the soft pad of a headphone against my ear. His voice seemed to come from another world. "She's turning goofy again, isn't she? Worse than ever."

◀ What does Kevin say to Leo through the headphone?

I stared at him through the glass. I put down the headphone and walked out.

I understood what he was doing. He had decided that it was now okay to say bad things about Stargirl. Permission to do so must have come from my behavior. Apparently the first to read me was Stargirl herself. I still felt the sting from her remark about the Ocotillo Ball.

---

words for everyday use

grav • i • tate (gra′ və tāt′) *vi.*, move toward something. *All the kids at the carnival seemed to <u>gravitate</u> toward the ferris wheel—it was by far the most popular ride.*

Was I that obvious?

* * *

Classrooms, hallways, courtyard, lunchroom—everywhere I went I heard her <u>disparaged</u>, mocked, slurred. Her attempt to become popular, to be more like them, had been a total failure. If anything, they detested her more now. And they were more vocal about it around me. Or was I just listening better?

She and Dori Dilson, the only Ukee Dooks, did a duet in the courtyard one day after school. Stargirl strummed the ukulele and they both sang "Blue Hawaii." Clearly, they had been practicing. They were very good. They were also very ignored. By the end of the song, they were the only two left in the courtyard.

Next day they were there again. This time they wore sombreros. They sang Mexican songs. "Cielito Lindo." "Vaya Con Dios, My Darling." I stayed inside the school. I was afraid to walk on past them, as if they weren't there. I was equally afraid to stand and listen. I peeked from a window. Stargirl was doing her best imitation of a flamenco;[1] the click of castanets came through the windowpane.

Students walked past, most of them not even glancing her way. I saw Wayne Parr and Hillari Kimble go past, Hillari laughing out loud. And Kevin. And the basketball guys. I realized now that the shunning would never end. And I knew what I should do. I should go out there and stand in front of them and applaud. I should show Stargirl and the world that I wasn't like the rest of them, that I appreciated her, that I celebrated her and her insistence on being herself. But I stayed inside. I waited until the last of the students had left the courtyard, and Stargirl and Dori were performing for no one. To my surprise they went on and on. It was too painful to watch. I left school by another door.

▶ Who is left standing by the end of the Ukee Dooks' song?

---

1. **flamenco.** Vigorous rhythmic dance style of the Andalusian Gypsies

words for everyday use

dis • par • age (di spar' əj) v., discredit; belittle. *Kevin refused to take Mia's theory seriously; instead he <u>disparaged</u> it.*

Chapter 31

As she had predicted, I did not ask her to the Ocotillo Ball. I did not ask anyone. I did not go.

She did.

The ball took place on a Saturday night in late May on the tennis courts of the Mica Country Club. When sunset was down to a faintly glowing ember in the west and the moon rose in the east, I went forth on my bicycle. I coasted by the club. Festooned with Cantonese lanterns,[1] the ball in the distance looked like a cruise ship at sea.

I could not identify individuals, only stirrings of color. Much of it was powder blue. The day after Wayne Parr said he had chosen powder blue for his dinner jacket, three-quarters of the boys ordered the same from Tuxedo Junction.

◄ What happened on the day after Wayne Parr chose a powder blue dinner jacket?

Back and forth I cruised in the night beyond the lights. Music reached my ears as random peeps. The desert flowers, so abundant in April, were dying now. I had the notion that they were calling to each other.

I cruised for hours. The moon rose into the sky like a lost balloon. Somewhere in the dark shapes of the Maricopas, a coyote howled.

In the days and weeks and years that followed, everyone agreed: they had never seen anything like it.

She arrived in a bicycle sidecar. Just big enough for her to sit in, the sidecar had a single outboard wheel. The inboard side was braced to the bike. Everything but the seat of the bike and the sidecar bench was covered in flowers. A ten-foot blanket of flowers trailed the rear fender like a bridal train. Palm fronds[2] flared from the handlebars. It looked like a float in the Rose Parade.[3] Dori Dilson pedaled the bicycle.

---

1. **Cantonese lanterns.** A Chinese style of lantern
2. **palm fronds.** Palm leaves
3. **Rose Parade.** Parade that takes place in Pasadena, California, in which all the floats are made entirely of roses

---

words for everyday use
fes • toon (fes tōōn′) v., adorn or hang with a wreath or garland of flowers. *The entire room was festooned with lilacs and lilies.*

Eyewitnesses later filled in what I could not see: parents' cameras flashing, floodlights making a second day as the gorgeous couples <u>disembark</u> from limos and borrowed convertibles and promenade to the festive courts. Showers of applause. Suddenly the flashing stops, the floodlights dim, a hush falls over the crowd. As a particularly long white limo rolls away from the entrance, here comes this three-wheeled bouquet.

▶ Who is the driver? What is she wearing?

The driver Dori Dilson wears a tailed white tuxedo and tall silk hat, but it is her passenger who rivets the crowd. Her strapless gown is a bright, rich yellow, as if pressed from buttercups. There must be one of those hooped contraptions underneath, for the skirt billows outward from her waist like an upside-down teacup. Her hair is incredible. Descriptions clash. Some say it is the color of honey, some say strawberries. It fluffs like a meringue high upon her head. It's a wig. No, it's all hers. Both sides are certain.

Earrings dangle. They are little silver somethings. But what? They are partly <u>obscured</u> by falling ringlets. Many answers are offered. The most popular is Monopoly pieces, but this will prove to be wrong.

From a rawhide string around her neck dangles a white inch-long banana-shaped fossil identifying her as a member in good standing of the Loyal Order of the Stone Bone.

▶ What kind of corsage is Stargirl wearing?

While others wear orchids, the corsage on her wrist is a small sunflower. Or a huge black-eyed Susan. Or some sort of daisy. No one is sure, except that the colors are yellow and black.

Before proceeding, she turns back to the bicycle and bends over a small basket hanging from the handlebars. The basket, too, is covered with flowers. She appears to kiss something in it. She then waves to Dori Dilson, Dori salutes, and the bicycle pulls away. People nearby catch a glimpse of tiny cinnamon-

---

words for everyday use

dis • em • bark (dis' im bärk') v., leave a means of transportation. *The older gentlemen disembarked from the taxi cab slowly.*

ob • scure (äb skyur') adj., unclear or unknown. *The obscure restaurant was known by few, which added to its charm.*

colored ears and two peppercorn eyes peering out of the basket.

"Beautiful."
 "Unusual."
 "Interesting."
 "Different."
 "Regal."
These words will come later from the parents lining the walk. For now, there are only stares as she makes her way from the entrance to the ball. Someone recalls a single camera flashing, but that is all. She is no one's child. She is the girl they have heard about. As she passes by she makes no attempt to avoid their eyes. On the contrary, she looks directly at them, turning to one side, then the other, looking into their eyes and smiling as if she knows them, as if they have shared grand and special things. Some turn aside, uneasy in a way they cannot account for; others feel suddenly empty when her eyes leave theirs. So distracting, so complete is she that she is gone before many realize that she had no escort, she was alone, a parade of one.

Perched on my bike in the distance, I remember looking up and seeing the torrent of stars we call the Milky Way. I remember wondering if she could see them, too, or were they lost in the light of the lanterns?

The dancing took place on the center tennis court, which had been covered with a portable parquet[4] floor. She did what everyone else did at the ball: she danced. To the music of Guy Greco and the Serenaders she danced the slow dances and the fast ones. She spread her arms wide and threw back her head and closed her eyes and gave every impression of thoroughly enjoying herself. They did not speak to her, of course, but they could not help looking over the shoulders of their dates. She clapped at the end of each number.

◄ How does Stargirl appear to be feeling while dancing alone on the dance floor?

---

4. **parquet.** A patterned wood surface

She's alone, they kept telling themselves, and surely she danced in no one's arms, yet somehow that seemed to matter less and less. As the night went on, and clarinet and coyote call mingled beyond the lantern light, the magic of their own powder-blue jackets and orchids seemed to fade, and it came to them in small sensations that they were more alone than she was.

Who was the first to crack? No one knows. Did someone brush against her at the punch table? Pluck a petal from her flower? (One was missing.) Whisper "Hi"? This much is certain: a boy named Raymond Studemacher danced with her.

To the student body at large, Raymond Studemacher did not have enough substance to trigger the opening of a supermarket door. He belonged to no team or organization. He took part in no school activities. His grades were ordinary. His clothing was ordinary. His face was ordinary. He had no <u>detectable</u> personality. Thin as a minute, he appeared to lack the <u>heft</u> to carry his own name. And in fact, when all eyes turned to him on the dance floor, those few who came up with a name for him frowned at his white jacket and whispered, "Raymond Something."

And yet there he was, Raymond Something, walking right up to her—it came out later that his date had suggested it—and speaking to her, and then they were dancing. Couples steered themselves to get a better look. At the end of the number, he joined her in clapping and returned to his date. He told her the silver earrings looked like little trucks.

Tension rose. Boys got antsy. Girls picked at their corsages. The ice shattered. Several boys broke from their dates. They were heading her way when she walked up to Guy Greco and said something to him. Guy Greco turned to the Serenaders, the baton flashed, and out came the sounds of that old teen dance standard: the bunny hop. Within seconds a

---

words for everyday use

de • tect • able (di tek′ tə bəl) *adj.*, able to be determined or noticed. *The light was* <u>*detectable*</u>*, but faint.*

heft (heft′) *n.*, weight, heaviness. *Compared to the kicker, the linebacker had much more* <u>*heft*</u>*.*

long line was snaking across the dance floor. Stargirl led the way. And suddenly it was December again, and she had the school in her spell.

Almost every couple joined in. Hillari Kimble and Wayne Parr did not.

◀ Who does not join in the bunny hop?

The line curled back and forth across the netless tennis courts. Stargirl began to improvise. She flung her arms to a make-believe crowd like a celebrity on parade. She waggled her fingers at the stars. She churned her fists like an egg-beater. Every action echoed down the line behind her. The three hops of the bunny became three struts of a vaudeville vamp.[5] Then a penguin waddle. Then a tippy-toed priss. Every new move brought new laughter from the line.

When Guy Greco ended the music, howls of protest greeted him. He restruck the downbeat.

To delighted squeals, Stargirl led them off the parquet dance floor onto the other courts—and then through the chain-link fence and off the tennis courts altogether. Red carnations and wrist corsages flashed as the line headed onto the practice putting green of the golf course. The line doodled around the holes, in and out of sidepools of lantern light. From the dance floor it seemed to be more than it was: one hundred couples, two hundred people, four hundred dancing legs seemed to be a single festive flowery creature, a fabulous millipede. And then there was less and less to see as the head vanished and the rest curled through the fringe of the light and followed, like the tail of a powder-blue dragon, into the darkness.

◀ Where does Stargirl lead the bunny hop?

One girl in chiffon had a tiff with her date and ran off toward the first tee, calling, "Wait for me!" She looked like a huge mint-green moth.

Their voices came in clearly from the golf course. The laughing and yelping made a raucous counterpoint to the metronomic *tock-tock-tock* of the bunny's

---

5. **vaudeville vamp.** Exaggerated strut of a vaudeville actress

---

words for everyday use

met • ro • nom • ic (me trə nä′ mik) *adj.*, mechanically regular. *The metronomic sound of the rain left me feeling tired.*

never-ending hop. Once, in the light of the quarter moon, they appeared in silhouette on a domed, distant green, like figures dancing in someone's dream.

And then quite suddenly they were gone, as if the dreamer had awakened. Nothing to see, nothing to hear. Someone called "Hey!" after them, but that was all.

It was, according to those left behind, like waiting for a diver in water to return to the surface. Hillari Kimble, for one, did not share that feeling. "I came here to dance," she declared. She pulled Wayne Parr along to the bandstand and demanded "regular music."

Guy Greco tilted his head to listen, but the baton did not stop and neither did the band.

In fact, as the minutes went by, the music seemed to become louder. Maybe it was an illusion. Maybe the band felt a connection to the dancers. Maybe the farther the line spun into the night, the louder the band had to play. Maybe the music was a tether. Or a kite string.

▶ What kind of dances do Hillari and Wayne try? What works?

Hillari Kimble dragged Wayne Parr out to the middle of the parquet floor. They slowdanced. They fastdanced. They even tried an old-fashioned jitterbug. Nothing worked. Nothing went with the triple-thumping drumbeat but the bunny hop itself. Hillari's orchid shed petals as she beat her fist on Wayne Parr's chest. "Do something!" she yelled. She ripped sticks of chewing gum from his pocket. She chewed them furiously. She split the wad and pressed the gum into her ears.

The band played on.

▶ How long do people think the bunny-hoppers were gone?

Afterward, there were many different guesses as to how long the bunny-hoppers were actually gone. Everyone agreed it seemed to be hours. Students stood under the last line of lanterns, their fingers curling through the plastic-coated wire of the fence, peering into the vast blackness, straining for a glimpse, a scrap of sound. All they heard was the call of a coyote. A boy dashed wildly into the darkness; he sauntered back, his blue jacket over his shoulder, laughing. A girl with glitter in her hair shivered. Her bare shoulders shook as if she were cold. She began to cry.

Hillari Kimble stalked along the fence, clenching and unclenching her fists. She could not seem to stand still.

When the call finally came—"They're back!"—it was from a lone watcher at the far end. A hundred kids—only Hillari Kimble stayed behind—turned and raced down eight tennis courts, pastel skirts flapping like stampeding flamingos. The fence buckled outward as they slammed into it. They strained to see. Light barely trickled over crusted earth beyond the fence. This was the desert side.

"Where? . . . Where?"

And then you could hear: whoops and yahoos out there, somewhere, clashing with the music. And then—*there!*—a flash of yellow, Stargirl leaping from the shadows. The rest followed out of the darkness, a long, powder-blue, many-headed birthing. *Hop-hop-hop.* They were still smack on the beat. If anything, they seemed more energized than before. They were fresh. Their eyes sparkled in the lantern light. Many of the girls wore browning, half-dead flowers in their hair.

Stargirl led them along the outside of the fence. Those inside got up a line of their own and hopped along. Guy Greco struck the downbeat three final times—*hop-hop-hop*—and the two lines collided at the gate in a frenzy of hugs and shrieks and kisses.

Shortly after, as the Serenaders gratefully played "Stardust," Hillari Kimble walked up to Stargirl and said, "You ruin everything." And she slapped her.

The crowd grew instantly still. The two girls stood facing each other for a long minute. Those nearby saw in Hillari's shoulders and eyes a flinching: she was waiting to be struck in reply. And in fact, when Stargirl finally moved, Hillari winced and shut her eyes. But it was lips that touched her, not the palm of a hand. Stargirl kissed her gently on the cheek. She was gone by the time Hillari opened her eyes.

◀ *What does Stargirl do after Hillari slaps her?*

Dori Dilson was waiting. Stargirl seemed to float down the promenade in her buttercup gown. She climbed into the sidecar, the flowered bicycle rolled off into the night, and that was the last any of us ever saw of her.

Chapter 32

That was fifteen years ago. Fifteen Valentine's Days.

I remember that sad summer after the Ocotillo Ball just as clearly as everything else. One day, feeling needy, empty, I walked over to her house. A For Sale sign pierced the ground out front. I peered through a window. Nothing but bare walls and floors.

I went to see Archie. Something in his smile said he had been expecting me. We sat on the back porch. Everything seemed as usual. Archie lighting his pipe. The desert golden in the evening sun. Señor Saguaro losing his pants.

Nothing had changed.

Everything had changed.

"Where?" I said.

A corner of his mouth winked open and a silky rumple of smoke emerged, paused as if to be admired, then drifted off past his ear. "Midwest. Minnesota."

"Will I ever see her again?"

He shrugged. "Big country. Small world. Who knows?"

"She didn't even finish out the school year."

"No."

"Just . . . <u>vamoosed</u>."

"Mm-hm."

"It's only been weeks, but it seems like a dream. Was she really here? Who was she? Was she real?"

He looked at me for a long time, his smile wry, his eyes twinkling. Then he shook his head as if coming out of a trance. He deadpanned, "Oh, you're waiting for an answer. What were the questions again?"

"Stop being nutty, Archie."

He looked off to the west. The sun was melting butter over the Maricopas. "Real? Oh, yes. As real as we get. Don't ever doubt that. That's the good news." He pointed the pipe stem at me. "And well named.

▶ Where does Archie say Stargirl has gone?

---

words for everyday use   va • moose (və müs′) v., depart quickly. *He <u>vamoosed</u> out of the room before I had a chance to say a proper good-bye.*

Stargirl. Though I think she had simpler things in mind. Star people are rare. You'll be lucky to meet another."

"Star people?" I said. "You're losing me here."

He chuckled. "That's okay. I lose myself. It's just my oddball way of accounting for someone I don't really understand any more than you do."

"So where do stars come in?"

He pointed the pipe stem. "The perfect question. In the beginning, that's where they come in. They supplied the ingredients that became us, the <u>primordial</u> elements. We are star stuff, yes?" He held up the skull of Barney, the Paleocene rodent. "Barney too, hm?"

I nodded, along for the ride.

"And I think every once in a while someone comes along who is a little more primitive than the rest of us, a little closer to our beginnings, a little more in touch with the stuff we're made of."

◀ What kind of person comes along every once in a while, according to Archie?

The words seemed to fit her, though I could not grasp their meaning.

He saw the <u>vacant</u> look on my face and laughed. He tossed Barney to me. He stared at me. "She liked you, boy."

The intensity of his voice and eyes made me blink. "Yes," I said.

"She did it for you, you know."

"What?"

"Gave up her self, for a while there. She loved you that much. What an incredibly lucky kid you were."

I could not look at him. "I know."

He shook his head with a wistful sadness. "No, you don't. You can't know yet. Maybe someday . . ."

I knew he was tempted to say more. Probably to tell me how stupid I was, how cowardly, that I blew the best chance I would ever have. But his smile returned, and his eyes were tender again, and nothing harsher than cherry smoke came out of his mouth.

---

words for everyday use

pri • mor • di • al (pri môr′ dē əl) adj., existing at the beginning; first in time. *The archaeologist uncovered <u>primordial</u> bones of perhaps the earliest humans yet discovered.*

va • cant (vā kənt) adj., not occupied; empty. *The lot had been <u>vacant</u> for years; now a house was being built on it.*

I continued to attend Saturday meetings of the Loyal Order of the Stone Bone. We did not speak of her again until the following summer, several days before I was to leave for college. Archie had asked me to come over.

He took me out back, but this time not to the porch. Instead he led me to the toolshed. He slid back the bolt and opened the door and—it was not a toolshed after all. "This was her office," he said and gestured for me to enter.

▶ What is in Archie's toolshed?

Here it was: all the stuff of her activity that I had expected to see in her room at home, the "office" whose location she would not reveal. I saw wheels of ribbon and wrapping paper, stacks of colored construction paper, cardboard boxes of newspaper clippings, watercolors and cans of paint, a yellow stack of phone books.

Tacked to one wall was a municipal map of Mica. Hundreds of pins of a dozen different colors pierced the map. There was no indication what they stood for. A huge homemade calendar covered the opposite wall. It had a square for every date in the year. Penciled into the squares were names. Across the top of the calendar was one word: BIRTHDAYS. There was one dot of color on the whole thing, a little red heart. It was next to my name.

▶ What is the title of the family album sort of book that Archie hands over to Leo?

Archie handed me a fat family album sort of book. The homemade title said "The Early Life of Peter Sinkowitz." I flipped through it. I saw the pictures she had taken that day: Peter squabbling with the little girls over his beloved banana roadster.

"I'm to wait five years, then give it to his parents," said Archie.

He pointed to a filing cabinet in the corner.

It had three drawers. I opened one. There were dozens of red hanging folders, each with a name tag sticking up. I saw "Borlock." Me. I pulled it out, opened it. There was the birthday notice that appeared in the *Mica Times* three years before. And a profile of me from the school paper. And pictures: candid snapshots of me in a parking lot, me leaving my house, me at the mall. Apparently, Peter Sinkowitz wasn't the only target for her camera. And a sheet of paper with two columns: "Likes" and "Doesn't Like." Heading the list of "Likes" was "porcupine neckties." Under that was "strawberry-banana smoothies."

I replaced my folder. I saw other names. Kevin. Dori Dillson. Mr. McShane. Danny Pike. Anna Grisdale. Even Hillari Kimble and Wayne Parr.

I stepped back. I was stunned.

"This is . . . unbelievable. Files. On people. Like she was a spy."

Archie nodded, smiling. "A lovely treason, hm?"

I could not speak. He led me out into the dazzling light.

Chapter 33

Throughout my college years I visited Archie whenever I came home. And then I got a job back East, and my visits were less frequent. As Archie grew older, the difference between himself and Señor Saguaro seemed to become less and less. We sat on the back porch. He seemed fascinated by my work. I had become a set designer. Only recently has it occurred to me that I became one on the day Stargirl took me to her enchanted place.

▶ When had Leo actually become a set designer?

On my last visit with him, he met me at the front door. He dangled keys in front of my eyes. "You drive."

An old tar pail rattled in the bed of his ancient pickup as he pointed me west to the Maricopas. In his lap he carried a brown paper bag.

Along the way I said, as I always did, "So, have you figured her out yet?"

It was years since she had gone, yet still we needed no name for her. We knew who we were talking about.

"I'm working on it," he said.

"What's the latest?"

We were following a familiar script.

On this day he stated: "She's better than bones." On my previous visit, he had said, "When a Stargirl cries, she does not shed tears, but light." On other days in other years, he had called her "the rabbit in the hat" and "the universal solvent" and "the recycler of our garbage."

He said these things with a sly grin, knowing they would <u>confound</u> me as I mulled them until our next meeting.

We were in the foothills by early afternoon. He directed me to stop on a stony shoulder of the road. We got out and walked. He brought the paper bag with him. I brought the pail. He pulled from it a

---

words for everyday use con • found (kən found') v., mix up indiscriminately; to baffle, stupefy, perplex, or confuse. *He was <u>confounded</u> when he found out about my unexpected decision to drop out of school.*

floppy blue hat, which he mashed onto his head. The sun that had looked warm and buttery at a distance was blazing hot here.

We didn't go far, as walking was a chore for him. We stopped at an outcropping of smooth, pale-gray rock. He pulled a small pick from the pail and tapped the rock. "This'll do," he said.

◀ In what does Archie gouge out a hole?

I held the paper bag while he put pick to rock. The skin on his arms had become dry and flaky, as if his body were preparing itself to rejoin the earth. It took him ten minutes to gouge out a hole that he judged to be right.

He asked for the bag. I was shocked at what he took from it.

"Barney!"

The skull of the Paleocene rodent.

"This is home," he said. He said he was sorry he did not have the energy to return Barney to his original <u>stratum</u> in South Dakota. He laid Barney in the hole, then took from his pocket a scrap of paper. He crumpled the scrap and stuffed it into the hole with the skull. Then he pulled a jug of water, a small bag of patching cement, a trowel, and a plastic tray from the tar pail. He mixed the cement and troweled over the hole. From a distance you wouldn't know the rock had been altered.

Heading back to the pickup, I asked him what was written on the paper.

"A word," he said. The way he said it told me I'd get no answer to the next question.

We rode east down out of the mountains and were home before sundown.

When I returned next time, someone else was living in Archie's house. The shed out back was gone. So was Señor Saguaro.

And a new elementary school now occupies Stargirl's enchanted place.

---

words for everyday use

strat • um (strā′ təm) n., sheetlike mass of sedimentary rock or earth of one kind lying between beds of other kinds. *You could see four distinct stratums in the earth, each layer of rock a different color.*

More Than Stars

▶ What is Kevin's occupation?

Since graduating, our class has had a reunion every five years, but I haven't yet gone. I stay in touch with Kevin. He never left Mica, has a family there now. Like me, he did not wind up in television, but he does make good use of his gift of gab: he's an insurance salesman.

Kevin says when the class gathers for reunions at the Mica Country Club, there is much talk of Stargirl and curiosity as to her whereabouts. He says the most common question these days is "Were you on the bunny hop?" At the last reunion several classmates, for a lark, lined up, hands to waists, and hopped around the putting green for a few minutes, but it wasn't the same.

No one is quite sure what happened to Wayne Parr, except that he and Hillari broke up shortly after graduation. The last anyone heard, he spoke of joining the Coast Guard.

The high school has a new club called the Sunflowers. To join, you have to sign an agreement promising to do "one nice thing per day for someone other than myself."

Today's Electron marching band is probably the only one in Arizona with a ukulele.

On the basketball court, the Electrons have never come close to the success they enjoyed when I was a junior. But something from that season has resurfaced in recent years that baffles fans from other schools. At every game, when the opposing team scores its first basket, a small group of Electron fans jumps to its feet and cheers.

Each time I visit Mica, I drive past her old house on Palo Verde. On the most recent visit, I saw a red-haired young man across the street, fixing water skis to the roof of a yellow Volkswagen Beetle. It must have been Peter Sinkowitz. I wondered if he was as possessive of his Beetle as he had been of the banana roadster. I wondered if he was old enough to love his scrapbook.

▶ What does Leo keep an eye open for?

As for me, I throw myself into my work and keep an eye peeled for silver lunch trucks, and I remember.

I sometimes walk in the rain without an umbrella. When I see change on the sidewalk, I leave it there. If no one's looking, I drop a quarter. I feel guilty when I buy a card from Hallmark. I listen for mockingbirds.

I read the newspapers. I read them from all over. I skip the front pages and headlines and go to the pages in back. I read the community sections and the fillers. I see little acts of kindness happening from Maine to California. I read of a man in Kansas City who stands at a busy intersection every morning and waves at the people driving to work. I read of a little girl in Oregon who sells lemonade in front of her house for five cents a cup—and offers a free back scratch to every customer.

◀ What does the little girl in Oregon sell?

When I read about things like these I wonder, *Is she there?* I wonder what she calls herself now. I wonder if she's lost her freckles. I wonder if I'll ever get another chance. I wonder, but I don't despair. Though I have no family of my own, I do not feel alone. I know that I am being watched. The echo of her laughter is the second sunrise I awaken to each day, and at night I feel it is more than stars looking down at me. Last month, one day before my birthday, I received a gift-wrapped package in the mail. It was a porcupine necktie.

Respond to the Selection

What effect has Stargirl had on Leo's life?

Investigate, Inquire, and Imagine

Recall: GATHERING FACTS

1a. What are Leo's first and second impulses after reading "Stargirl Loves Leo" posted on the road-runner?

2a. How does Leo react to Stargirl's transformation into Susan?

3a. What does Susan (Stargirl) do after Mr. McShane stops the car on the way to the oratorical contest? What does she ask Mr. McShane when she returns to the car?

4a. Stargirl tells Leo that she knows he's not going to take her to the Ocotillo Ball, but that it's okay. What kind of smile does Stargirl then give Leo? What effect does her smile have on Leo?

Interpret: FINDING MEANING

➤ 1b. Explain his impulses.

➤ 2b. Why do you think he feels this way?

➤ 3b. What emotions do you think Susan is releasing after she gets out of the car? What effect does what Susan hears and/or sees seem to have on her?

➤ 4b. Why does Leo feel that way in that moment?

Analyze: TAKING THINGS APART

5a. Find examples of how "Susan" attempts to be a "somebody" instead of a "nobody."

Synthesize: BRINGING THINGS TOGETHER

➤ 5b. Is Susan successful in becoming a somebody? Explain your answer.

Evaluate: MAKING JUDGMENTS

6a. After Susan returns from the oratorical contest, she makes the change back to Stargirl. When Leo sees Stargirl and Dori in the courtyard singing, he feels he should go out and applaud Stargirl's insistence on being herself and show the world that he appreciates Stargirl for who she is. Instead he waits until the courtyard is empty and leaves the school. What do you think of Leo's decision? Explain your answer.

Extend: CONNECTING IDEAS

6b. If a girl or boy similar to Stargirl's character came to your school, what do you think would happen? Do you think your peers would react the way the characters in the story did? Would you try to make friends with this new student? Explain.

Understanding Literature

IRONY OF SITUATION. **Irony of situation** is an event that contradicts the expectations of the characters, the reader, or the audience of a literary work. Reread the section in chapter 25 when Leo is giving examples of kinds of groups in which people belong, like families, a town, or a country. What example does Stargirl come up with? What is ironic about her example?

THEME. A **theme** is a central idea in a literary work. Identify three events or indications of the theme of individuality in this novel. What statement is made about individuality?

RESOLUTION. The **resolution** is the point at which the central conflict is ended, or resolved. What event marks the resolution in this novel?

Plot Analysis of
Stargirl

The following diagram, known as a Plot Pyramid, illustrates the main plot of *Stargirl*. For definitions and more information on the parts of a plot illustrated below, see the Handbook of Literary Terms on page 198.

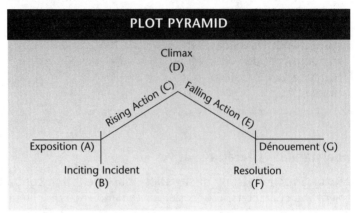

PLOT PYRAMID

The parts of a plot are as follows:

The **exposition** is the part of a plot that provides background information about the characters, setting, or conflict.

The **inciting incident** is the event that introduces the central conflict.

The **rising action**, or complication, develops the conflict to a high point of intensity.

The **climax** is the point of highest interest and suspense in a literary work.

The **falling action** is all the events that follow the climax.

The **resolution** is the point at which the central conflict is ended, or resolved.

The **dénouement** is any material that follows the resolution and that ties up loose ends.

Exposition (A)

Leo describes how he was given the porcupine necktie for his birthday from a mysterious person. Leo meets Stargirl on the first day of school. Stargirl dances on the football field, joins the cheerleading squad, sings Happy Birthday to students in school, and becomes the most popular girl in school. She goes on to win the school oratorical contest.

Inciting Incident (B)

Students learn that Stargirl attended a funeral of someone she didn't know and gave a boy a bike after he had an accident. Stargirl cheers for the other team during the basketball games. Stargirl goes on *Hot Seat* and the jurors attack her character and her actions of the past few weeks. The jurors question Stargirl's way of doing things.

Rising Action (C)

Stargirl comes to the aid of a player from the opposite team after he is hurt during a basketball game. At the end of the game, a student throws a ripe tomato at her. Stargirl sends Leo a card that says she loves him. Leo seeks out Stargirl, going to her house at night to try to catch a glimpse of her. Students at the school start to shun Stargirl and Leo.

Climax (D)

Stargirl wants to fit in and get the acceptance of the other students, so she loses her "Stargirl-ways," takes the name Susan, dresses like the other girls at school, and tries to act "normal."

Falling Action (E)

Stargirl has a vision in which she wins the state oratorical contest and is accepted by the other students. She does win the contest, but no one is waiting for her at school to offer their congratulations, other than Dori.

Resolution (F)

Stargirl returns to acting like herself. She stops pretending to be someone she is not and embraces her own values and beliefs.

Dénouement (G)

Stargirl goes to the Ocotillo Ball without Leo. All of the students in attendance of the dance, except Hillari and Wayne, come to accept Stargirl for who she is and join her in the bunny hop. Leo rejects Stargirl, knowing she will never truly be like his classmates, but grows up to regret his decision.

"The Origin of Plumage"
Iroquois myth recorded by Erminnie A. Smith
in *Myths of the Iroquois*

ABOUT THE RELATED READING

Erminnie Smith (1836–1886) was a geologist and an anthropologist hired by the Smithsonian Institution to collect information about the Iroquois people in 1880. She gathered Iroquois myths and legends and learned about the Iroquois language. The myths and legends appeared in the book *Myths of the Iroquois,* which was published in 1883. They range from stories about the origin of humans and other things on earth to stories about supernatural beings and tales about humans interacting with animals.

The Origin of Plumage

In the beginning, the birds, having been created without feathers, remained hidden. They were ashamed of their appearance. One day they assembled in a great meeting. They asked their gods to give them some kind of covering. They were told that these coverings were all ready but that they were a long distance away. The birds must send for them.

◀ *Why did the gods tell the birds about the coverings?*

Accordingly, another meeting was held to encourage some bird to go in search of the plumage.[1] However, each bird had some excuse for not going. At last, a turkey buzzard volunteered to go and to bring back the feathers. It was a long journey, but the bird was directed on his way by the gods.

Finally, the turkey buzzard found the coverings. He selfishly took the most beautiful one for himself. However, he found that he could not fly in this covering. He continued to try on all of the feathered uniforms until he selected his present suit. This covering, although the least beautiful of all, allowed him to glide gracefully through the air. The good turkey buzzard returned and brought with him all of the feathery garments. Each bird chose his present colored suit.

◀ *What is the turkey buzzard's covering like?*

---

1. **plumage.** Feathers

Critical Thinking

1. Identify one theme of this writing.
2. Compare the teachings of this myth with Stargirl's outlook on appearance. How are they the same? How are they different?

"Passports to Understanding"
by Maya Angelou
from her collection of essays,
Wouldn't Take Nothing for My Journey Now

ABOUT THE RELATED READING

Maya Angelou, born in 1928, is a well-loved poet and writer. She also worked with Dr. Martin Luther King Jr. for the Southern Christian Leadership Conference, an organization dedicated to using nonviolent protest to end racism and achieve civil rights for African Americans. According to Angelou, there is a basic message in all her work: "What I try to say is that as human beings we are more alike than we are unalike."

In *Wouldn't Take Nothing for My Journey Now,* a book of essays, Angelou offers her ideas about her life, about serving and giving to others, and about celebrating people. A theme that runs through the essays is that all people need to practice tolerance and understanding of others.

Passports to Understanding

Human beings are more alike than unalike, and what is true anywhere is true everywhere, yet I encourage travel to as many destinations as possible for the sake of education as well as pleasure.

It is necessary, especially for Americans, to see other lands and experience other cultures. The American, living in this vast country and able to <u>traverse</u> three thousand miles east to west using the same language, needs to hear languages as they collide in Europe, Africa, and Asia.

A tourist, browsing in a Paris shop, eating in an Italian *ristorante,* or idling along a Hong Kong street,

◄ *According to Angelou, what does the American need to hear?*

words for everyday use tra • verse (tra vərs') *v.,* travel across or move through. *Henry <u>traversed</u> the crowded downtown, dangerously weaving in and out of traffic on his bicycle.*

will encounter three or four languages as she negotiates the buying of a blouse, the paying of a check, or the choosing of a trinket. I do not mean to suggest that simply overhearing a foreign tongue adds to one's understanding of that language. I do know, however, that being exposed to the existence of other languages increases the perception that the world is populated by people who not only speak differently from oneself but whose cultures and philosophies are other than one's own.

▶ *What can travel do?*

Perhaps travel cannot prevent bigotry,[1] but by demonstrating that all people cry, laugh, eat, worry, and die, it can introduce the idea that if we try to understand each other, we may even become friends.

Critical Thinking

1. How do you think Maya Angelou would react to Stargirl? Do you think they would be friends? Explain your answers.
2. According to Angelou, what kinds of things do tourists learn while browsing, idling, or eating in another country? In what way is this philosophy similar to the random acts of kindness that Stargirl performs for strangers?
3. Maya Angelou values travel because it helps people understand each other. Do you think Stargirl shares this value? Leo? Explain your answers.

---

1. **bigotry.** Devotion to one's own beliefs and prejudices

"New Love"
by Eve Merriam

ABOUT THE RELATED READING

Eve Merriam (1916–1992) was one of the most celebrated poets of the 20th century. She also wrote and directed plays, taught in colleges, and gave many lectures. She wrote poetry both for adults and children. The poem "New Love" is from a collection entitled *Fresh Paint*. The poems in that book are about familiar things and experiences, such as love, friendship, mushrooms, snow, and new shoes.

New Love

I am telling my hands
not to blossom into roses

I am telling my feet
not to turn into birds
and fly over rooftops

and I am putting a hat on my head
so the flaming meteors
in my hair
will hardly show

◄ *Why is the speaker putting a hat on?*

Critical Thinking

1. What is the mood of this poem?
2. How does the speaker of this poem compare to Stargirl? to Leo? Explain.
3. What advice might Stargirl give the speaker of this poem? What advice might Leo give the speaker?

from *Pay It Forward*
by Catherine Ryan Hyde

ABOUT THE RELATED READING

Catherine Ryan Hyde published the novel *Pay It Forward* in 2000. The book is about a twelve-year-old boy who sets out to change the world by dishing out kindness to people. The story reflects the idea that humans are naturally good and when given the chance, will work hard to prove it.

Shortly after the book's publication, Hyde started the Pay It Forward Foundation. The foundation provides start-up funds for youth kindness projects, offers learning materials for school projects, and sponsors awards for school projects. Hyde says, "I didn't write the novel expecting a social movement, but it's certainly been exciting to watch it grow." Hyde began a Pay It Forward Movement Internet site as a place to collect real-life stories about people doing good deeds. In 2001, *Pay It Forward* became a movie, starring Kevin Spacey, Helen Hunt and Haley Joel Osment.

from *Pay It Forward*

Maybe someday I'll have kids of my own. I hope so. If I do, they'll probably ask what part I played in the movement that changed the world. And because I'm not the person I once was, I'll tell them the truth. My part was nothing. I did nothing. I was just the guy in the corner taking notes.

▶ *Who is the narrator in this section?*

My name is Chris Chandler and I'm an investigative reporter. Or at least I was. Until I found out that actions have consequences, and not everything is under my control. Until I found out that I couldn't change the world at all, but a seemingly ordinary twelve-year-old boy could change the world completely—for the better, and forever— working with nothing but his own altruism, one good idea, and a couple of years. And a big sacrifice. And a splash of publicity. That's where I came in.

I can tell you how it all started. It started with a teacher who moved to Atascadero, California to teach social studies to junior high school students. A teacher nobody knew very well, because they couldn't get past his face. Because it was hard to look at his face.

It started with a boy who didn't seem all that remarkable on the outside, but who could see past his teacher's face. It started with an assignment that the teacher had given out a hundred times before, with no startling results. But that assignment in the hands of that boy caused a seed to be planted, and after that nothing in the world would ever be the same. Nor would anybody want it to be. And I can tell you what it became. In fact, I'll tell you a story that will help you understand how big it grew.

◄ What is this narrator going to tell the reader about?

About a week ago my car stalled in the middle of a busy intersection, and it wouldn't start again no matter how many times I tried. I'd been expecting this. It was an old car. It was as good as gone.

A man came up behind me, a stranger.

"Let's get it off to the side of the road," he said. "Here. I'll help you push." When we got it—and ourselves—to safety he handed me the keys to his car. A nice silver Acura, barely two years old. "You can have mine," he said. "We'll trade."

He didn't give me the car as a loan. He gave it to me as a gift. He took my address, so he could send me the title. And he did send the title; it just arrived today.

"A great deal of generosity has come into my life lately," the note said, "so I felt I should take your old car and use it as a trade-in. I can well afford something new, so why not give as good as I've received?"

◄ What did the note say?

That's what the world has become. No, actually it's more. It's become even more. It's not just the kind of world in which a total stranger will give me his car as a gift. It's become the kind of world in which the day I received that gift was not dramatically different from all other days. Such generosity has become the way of things. It's become commonplace.

◄ What has generosity become?

So, this much I understand well enough to relate: It started as an extra credit assignment for a social studies class and turned into a world where no one goes hungry, no one is cold, no one is without a job or a ride or a loan.

Reuben St. Clair was the teacher who started it all. He was closer to Trevor than anybody except maybe Trevor's mother, Arlene. So, after the fact, when it was my job to write books about the movement, I asked Reuben two important questions.

"What was it about Trevor that made him different?" I asked.

Reuben thought carefully and then said, "The thing about Trevor was that he was just like everybody else, except for the part of him that wasn't."

Then I asked, "When you first handed out that now-famous assignment, did you think that one of your students would actually change the world?"

And Reuben replied, "No, I thought they all would. But perhaps in smaller ways."

So now that you know how big it got in the long run, let's go back to an earlier part of the story. Trevor's mother decides she wants to know more about the project Trevor brought home from social studies class. She goes in to school to talk to his teacher, Mr. St. Clair. She doesn't know yet that he is an African-American Vietnam vet with a face badly scarred from the war.

First of all—though it wasn't the most important part—he was black. She did not feel so very different about black people—it wasn't that. It was more that she tried so hard to bend over backwards to show she wasn't like that. So he looked up, and she still had nothing to say. And not mostly over any racial issues, either, but more because she had never seen a man with only half a face. She moved through the room, toward his desk, feeling small, feeling like twenty-five years ago, when these desks were too big to fit her. And he was still waiting for something to be said.

Arlene asked, "What's Paying Forward?"

"Excuse me?"

"That expression. Paying Forward. What does it mean?"

"I give up. What does it mean?" He seemed mildly curious toward her, slightly amused, and as a result, miles above her, making her feel small and ignorant. He was a big man, and not only in physical stature, although that too.

"That's what you are supposed to tell me."

"I would love to, madam, if I knew. If you don't mind my asking, who are you?"

▶ What was the narrator's first important question for Reuben?

▶ What is Reuben's answer to the narrator's second question?

"Oh, did I forget to say that? Excuse me. Arlene McKinney." She reached her hand out and he shook it. Trying not to look at his face, she noticed that his left arm was deformed somehow, the wrong size, which gave her the shivers for just a second. "My boy is in your Social Studies class. Trevor."

◀ What is Arlene trying not to do? What does she notice?

Something came onto his face then, a positive recognition, which, being connected in some way to her boy, made her like this man better. "Trevor, yes. I like Trevor. I particularly like him. Very honest and direct."

Arlene tried for a little sarcastic laugh, but it came out a snort, a pig sound, and she could feel her face turn red because of it. "Yeah, he's all of that alright. Only you say it like it's a good thing."

"It is, I think. Now what's this about Paying Forward? I'm supposed to know something about that?"

"It has something to do with an assignment you gave out. That's what Trevor said. He said it was a project for your Social Studies class."

"Ah, yes. The Assignment." He moved to the blackboard, and she swung out of his way, as though there were a big wind around him that kept her from getting too close. "I'll write it out for you, exactly as I did for the class. It's very simple." And he did.

THINK OF AN IDEA FOR WORLD CHANGE, AND PUT IT INTO ACTION

He set his chalk down, and turned back. "That's all it is. This Paying Forward must be Trevor's own idea."

◀ What does Reuben say must be Trevor's own idea?

"That's all it is? That's all? You just want them to change the world. That's all. Well, I'm glad you didn't give them anything hard."

"Mrs. McKinney—"

"Miss McKinney, I am on my own. Now you listen here. Trevor is twelve years old. And you want him to change the world. I never heard such bull."

"First of all, it's a voluntary assignment. For extra credit. If a student finds the idea overwhelming, he or she need not participate. Second of all, what I want is for the students to re-examine their role in the world, and think of ways one person can make a difference. It's a very healthy exercise."

"So is climbing Mount Everest, but that might be too much for the poor little guy, too."

▶ What seems odd to Reuben?

So later, because Mr. St. Clair knew that Trevor's mother was a little bit mad, it seemed odd to him when Trevor delivered a message that was supposed to be from Arlene.

"I want to talk to you," Trevor said, turning and stopping in front of Reuben's desk. He jammed his hands deep into his pockets and waited until the last of the other students had gone. Little sweeps of his eyes and a slight rocking on his heels revealed something, but Reuben wasn't sure he could properly decipher it. A little nervousness, maybe.

Finally, convinced that they were alone, Trevor said, "My mom wants to know if you'll come to dinner tomorrow night."

"She said that?"

"Yeah. She said that."

And that little place in Reuben, the one he could never properly train, jumped up to meet her kindness, despite his warnings. Maybe she didn't dislike him as much as he thought. But even Reuben's heart could sense when something didn't fit.

"Why does she want me to come to dinner?"

"I dunno. Why not? Maybe she wants to talk about my project."

"Couldn't we have a little private parent-teacher conference here at school?"

"Oh. Here at school. Well. I asked her. But she said, you know. She works so hard and all. Two jobs. She just said it would be nice if you could come over."

"I guess that would be okay. What time?"

"Uh. I'll have to ask her. I'll let you know tomorrow."

▶ What had Reuben been right about?

Reuben had been right. She was still a little mad, and there was something suspicious about that invitation. Reuben found this out when she came to see him again the next day.

A beam of morning sun slanting through the window caught Arlene and made her brighter than anything else in the room, glowing on a strip of bare midriff below her lacy tank top. Untanned, vulnerable skin, like a china doll. And she was pretty, but not the kind that made him hurt.

"Why did you tell my boy we had to meet at my house?"

"I didn't. I didn't say we had to meet at all."

"You didn't? Trevor told me to make chicken fajitas because you were coming for dinner. Because you wanted to talk to me about his project."

"Really?" Interesting. "He told me that you invited me over for dinner, and he thought it was because you wanted to talk to me about his project."

"But why not here at school?"

"He said you work two jobs, and it would be easier if I came to the house."

"I'm here, aren't I?"

"I'm only telling you what he said."

"Oh. Okay. Why's he trying to get you over, then?"

It would be a risk to say it, but Reuben guessed that he probably would anyway. "Yesterday morning he asked me if I was married. And then he asked me if I'd like to be."

◀ What had Trevor asked Reuben the day before?

"So?"

"I'm just <u>speculating</u>."

"He was probably just curious. I'm telling you that kid don't never know when to keep shut."

"I just thought . . ."

"What?"

"I just thought he might be trying to fix us up."

"Us? You must be joking."

"I realize we're the world's most unlikely couple, but, after all, he is just a boy."

"Trevor would never do such a thing. He knows his daddy is gonna come home."

"Just speculating."

"I know you don't like me."

He was surprised to hear her say it, especially as he admired her. "What makes you think that?"

---

words for everyday use spec • u • late (spek' yü lāt) v., take to be true without solid evidence. *Jackson <u>speculated</u> that the tall dun stallion would win the race, only because he looked unusually tall and athletic.*

She made that noise again, that rude little snort. "You just said we're the most unlikely couple in the world. What does that mean, if you're not looking down on me?"

Reuben thought, It means I assumed you were looking down on me. It means I knew you were thinking it, so I had to say it. But Reuben couldn't bring himself to give those answers, so she went on.

"You think I'm too stupid to see the way you look down on me? Well, I may not have your education, and I may not talk good like you, but that don't mean I'm stupid."

"I never said you were stupid."

"You didn't have to."

"I never thought it either. I think you're being overly sensitive."

"What do you know about what I'm feeling?"

"When it comes to oversensitivity, I'm something of an expert. Anyway, none of this was my idea, and if you don't want me in your house I won't come."

"Uh, no, truth is . . ." Reuben knew from the pause, from the strain in her face, that if she ever finished this sentence she'd tell him something difficult. Something that was hard for her to say to anyone, but particularly to him. "Truth is, I'm not doing so good talking to him about this. I could use the help. Six o'clock?"

So Reuben went to Trevor and Arlene's house.

▶ What does Reuben remember about arriving at Trevor and Arlene's home?

Reuben remembers: "She answered the door looking distressingly nice. She was wearing this blousy, cottony dress in a flower print, as if she took dinner guests rather seriously. I stepped into her living room, holding flowers that I couldn't bring myself to give her. Frozen. Every part of me frozen. For the longest time neither of us could seem to talk about anything. And then Trevor showed up, thank God."

* * *

As soon as Arlene cleared the dinner dishes from the table, Trevor ran to his room and got his calculator. He'd put off explaining his project, all through dinner, because, he said, it was too hard to explain without a calculator.

"This all started with something Daddy taught me."

Arlene's ears perked up at that, and she pulled her chair around, as if to watch the calculator over his shoulder.

"Remember that riddle he used to do? Remember that, Mom?"

"Well, I don't know, honey. He knew a lot of riddles."

"Remember that one about working for thirty days?"

"No, Trevor, I don't think I do."

"Remember, he said if you were going to work for somebody for thirty days, and you had a choice: you could take a hundred dollars a day, or you could take a dollar the first day, and then it would be doubled every day. I said I'd take a hundred dollars a day. But he said I'd lose out. So I worked it out on my calculator. A hundred dollars a day for thirty days is three thousand dollars. But if you double that dollar every day, you'd make over five hundred million on your last day. Not to mention everything between. That's how I thought of my idea for Mr. St. Clair's class. You see, I do something real good for three people. And then when they ask how they can pay it back, I say they have to Pay It Forward. To three more people. Each. So nine people get helped. Then those people have to do twenty-seven." He turned on the calculator, punched in a few numbers. "Then it sort of spreads out, see. To eighty-one. Then two hundred forty-three. Then seven hundred twenty-nine. Then two thousand, one hundred eighty-seven. See how big it gets?"

"But, honey. There's just one little problem with that."

"What, Mom?"

"I'm sure Mr. St. Clair will explain it to you."

Reuben jumped at the mention of his name. "I will?"

"Yes. Tell him what's wrong with the plan."

She fixed him with a look that burned in silence.

Reuben thought, I'm sorry, Miss McKinney, if you want your son to believe that people are basically

◀ What is the riddle that Trevor's father had taught him?

selfish and <u>unresponsive</u>, you'll have to tell him so yourself. Reuben smiled tightly and shook his head, saying nothing.

"Well, Trevor," she said. "I think it's a good project. Tell us some more about it."

So Trevor explained, with the help of his calculator, how big this thing could become. Somewhere around the sixteenth level, at which he'd involved forty-three million, forty-six thousand, seven hundred twenty-one people, the calculator proved smaller than Trevor's <u>optimism</u>. But he was convinced that in just a few more levels the numbers would be larger than the population of the world. "Then you know what happens? Then everybody gets helped more than once. And then it gets bigger even faster."

"What do you think, Mr. St. Clair?" Arlene clearly wanted something from him, but he wasn't sure from minute to minute what that something might be.

"I think it's a <u>noble</u> idea, Trevor. A big effort. Big efforts lead to good grades."

Now Trevor's big effort already had three big ideas. Three people he was going to help to get started. Reuben was one—he'd been right about that. Trevor really was trying to fix him up with Arlene. Another was Jerry, a homeless man who had some problems with drugs.

He spent the night in a dumpster, behind the auto parts store, not two blocks from the place he planned to be at nine a.m. Even in his sleep, there was hopefulness. Something he'd been missing for awhile.

When he'd first read it, it had made him feel so good. So he read it again.

It was in his shirt pocket, folded. The newsprint smeared by the sweat of his hands. Rumpled. But he could read it just the same.

▶ *Of what is Trevor convinced?*

▶ *What does Jerry, the homeless man, read? What does it say?*

FREE MONEY AND OTHER HELP FOR SOMEONE DOWN ON LUCK. COME TO CORNER TRAFFIC WAY AND EL CAMINO REAL. SATURDAY MORNING 9:00.

He couldn't get the feeling back, though. And maybe because he didn't feel it anymore, maybe that's why he'd come to this, why he'd sunk so low.

But he set off just the same. But before he even got to the corner he saw he was late. Later than he thought. There were seventeen people already there.

They were almost all men, he noticed, waiting; the one exception was a woman with no front teeth. Some looked better than he did, some worse. He had that thought, then doubted it. Doubted his own perception of how he looked. It had been awhile since he'd looked in a mirror.

And then it hit him.

I'm looking in a mirror right now.

A boy twelve, thirteen years old rode up on a bike, an old beach cruiser. The kid looked at the crowd. The crowd looked at him. Then he said, "Holy cow. Are you all here for the ad?"

A few people nodded.

◀ What does Trevor say he wanted?

"Holy cow." He said it again. Shook his head. "I only wanted one guy."

Then this big bald guy walked up. Said, "You did that ad?"

"Yeah, I did."

"Well, that's it, then." And almost everybody left. Jerry could hear them grumbling, "Shoulda knowed it was all a gag, real funny, kid."

The kid just stood there awhile. Kind of relieved, Jerry thought, because now there were only a few left. Jerry walked up to the kid. Nice. Humble, not like to scare him. "So, is it a joke?"

◀ What does Trevor tell Jerry?

"No, it's for real. I got a paper route, and I make thirty-five dollars a week, and I want to give it to somebody. Who'll, like, get a job and not need it after a while. Just to get 'em started, you know? Like food and something better to wear, and some bus fare. Or whatever."

And somebody behind Jerry, some voice over his shoulder said, "Yeah, but which somebody?"

Yeah. That was the problem.

▶ What does Trevor ask the people to do?

The kid thought this over for a bit. Then he said he had some paper in his bookbag, and he asked everybody to write out why they thought it should be them.

And when he said that, six people left.

Kid said, "I wonder what happened to them?"

And the lady with no front teeth, she said, "What makes you think everybody can write?"

It was clear from the look on the kid's face that he never would have thought of that.

Here's what Jerry wrote:

Why I think I deserve the money, by Jerry Busconi:

Well, for starters, I will not say I deserve it better than anybody. Because, who is to say? I am not a perfect person, and maybe somebody else will say they are. And you are a smart kid. I bet you are. And you will know they are handing you a line. I am being honest. I know you said you wanted somebody down on his luck. But you know what? It is all bull. Luck has nothing to do with this. Look at all these people who showed up today. We are a bunch of bums. They will say it is bad luck. But I won't sell you a line, kid. We did this to ourselves.

I lost some stuff because of my problems. A car, even though it was not a very good one. And my apartment. And then I went to jail, and they did not hold my job for when I got out.

But I got lots of things I can do. I got skills. I have worked in wrecking yards, and in body shops, and I have even worked as a mechanic. I am a good mechanic. It's not that I'm not. But, used to, you could go in kind of scruffy and dirty. For a mechanics job no one would mind.

▶ What problem does Jerry encounter when he applies for a job?

But now times is hard, and guys show up for the same job. Dressed good, and some even got a state license. So they say, fill out this form. Which I can do. Cause as you see, I can read and write pretty good. But then they say, put down your number. We'll call you if you get the job. But the dumpster where I been staying ain't got a phone. So I say, I'm just getting settled in. And they say, put your address, then. We'll send you a postcard.

And they know, then. That you are on the street. And I guess they figure you got problems, stuff they don't know nothing about.

And, well, I guess I do. Like I said.

But if I had a chance at a job now, I would not screw it up like I have done before. It would be different this time.

These other people, look at them. They have got used to their situation. They expect to sleep on the street. And I guess that is okay with them.

But it is not okay with me. I don't think I quite sunk that low. Anyway, not yet.

So if you go with me, you won't be sorry. I guess that's all I got to say.

Also, thank you. I never knowed no kid who gave money away. I had a job at your age, and I spent the money on me. You must be a good kid.

I guess that's all now. Thanks for your time.

When Jerry looked up, everybody else, except the kid, had gone.

So Trevor chooses Jerry to help. Trouble is, Arlene's not very happy having him around the house.

◀ Who does Trevor choose to help? What trouble does this cause?

He'd gone into the garage. Rolled out an old oriental rug in a corner. Against a wall. Barely got his eyes closed. She came in, flipped on the lights. Made him blink.

"It's only me, ma'am. Jerry. Just takin' a quick break. Just a nap. Then I'll get some more work done on your truck."

"I know you been living here, in my garage."

"No, ma'am. Just a quick nap."

"Then where are you staying?"

"Down at the shop where I work. They let me sleep on the couch in the waiting room."

"Get up, I'll drive you down there."

Getting into her car, her in the driver's seat, the dome light on as he got in beside her, he saw her face clear. Looking at her, he thought, you and me, we're not so very different and maybe you know it. But he knew better than to say it out loud.

◀ What does Jerry think as he looks at Arlene?

They drove in silence down The Camino, a ghost town at this hour.

Jerry said, "I know you don't like me."

"It's not that."

"What, then?"

"Look, Jerry, I'm trying to raise that boy on my own. No help from nobody. I can't watch him all the time."

"I don't mean no harm to your son."

"You don't mean none."

She pulled up in front of the Quicky Lube & Tune. It was cold out there. He didn't want to get out.

"Thanks for the ride, ma'am."

"I don't have anything against you personally. I don't."

"Right. Whatever."

He stepped out of the warm car. Into the wind. A minute later she was behind him.

"Look, Jerry. In a different world, who knows. We could have been friends even. It's just that—"

"Pleased to hear you say that, ma'am. The way you been acting, I'da thought only one of us is people."

"I never meant that."

"Never meant it."

▶ What do both Jerry and Arlene see in the sky?

She turned to go back to the car. He turned to watch her go. So they both saw it. Like a long streak, starting at the top of the sky. Drifting down, but fast. Lighting up the night like lightning. A ball of fire with a tail.

"Holy cow," she said. "Did you see that? What was that, a comet?"

▶ What does Jerry say about falling stars?

"Meteor maybe, I don't know. When I was a kid, we used to call that a falling star. I used to think if you saw one, you'd get your wish. You know, like all your dreams'd come true?"

She turned back to look at him. All softness in her face. Maybe it had never occurred to her that bums used to be kids. Or wanted their dreams to come true, like everybody.

"Well, good luck."

"Ma'am?"

"What?"

"I get my first paycheck today. And I'll go get a cheap room. Be out of your hair. Your boy won't be sorry he made the effort. I don't think you will either. I'll do just what I'm supposed to do. Pass it along, you know."

"Will you explain to me about that? How that Paying Forward thing goes?"

He kind of blinked. "Didn't he tell you?"

"Yeah, but I'd kinda like to hear what it means for you."

Jerry remembers, "So, I explained Paying Forward to her. I got me a stick. Sketched it out in the dirt. In the dark. I drew them three circles. And explained them. Like the kid explained them to me. 'See, this one. That's me.' I said that. 'These other two, I don't know. Two other somebodies, I guess. That he's gonna help. See, the trick is, it's something big. A big help. Like you wouldn't do for just anybody. Maybe your mother or your sister. But not nobody else. He does that for me. I got to do it for three others. Other two, they got to do for three others. Those nine others, they got to do it for three others. Each. That makes twenty-seven.'

◄ How does Jerry describe a "big help"?

"Now, I ain't so good with math. But that kid, he worked it out. It gets real big, real fast. Like you can't believe how fast. Up in the thousands in no time.

"So, I'm on my knees there. Drawing all these circles in the dirt. Counting by threes. Running out of dirt. You can't believe how fast. And you know, it happened again. And we both saw it. A big comet, or whatever. Did I mention about that first comet we saw? I guess I did. So we see another comet. Falling star. Falling, shooting, I don't know. But I ain't never seen two, all in one night. It was kind of spooky.

"We're looking at these circles, thinking this whole thing could be great. Except it won't be. Because, well we all know it won't. Because people, they are no good. They won't really Pay It Forward. They will take your help but that's all.

"I know we were both thinking that. And then the sky lit up again. That big comet. The second one, I mean. I ain't sayin' there was a third. Maybe I made it sound that way. But two, anyway. That's a lot. Spooky.

"You know, it's a big world out there. Bigger than we think. After awhile it was all the same stuff we was saying. Over and over. But I liked it anyway. After awhile she went home. But after that, the night was, like...different. Like...not so...you know...cold. Or something.

And then the third person was an old woman Trevor knew from his paper route. She had arthritis and couldn't do her own gardening anymore, so Trevor did it for her— for free.

Lately Mrs. Greenberg had begun to dream of waking up, stretching and flexing through the pain in her arthritic joints, easing to the window to discover that, as if by magic, the garden was once again whole. And now, in the dusk of a cool spring evening, the garden was whole. Trimmed, the grass mowed, beds laid with fresh cedar chips, freshly raked, bags of leaves and trimmings bundled at the curb, soon to be trash-day history.

Not an unexplained miracle, exactly, because she'd watched the neighbor boy do it all, day after day. Barely a head taller than he, she'd stood at his side and shown him the junctions at which rose bushes begged to be trimmed, and the aphids to be sprayed, and the weeds that had to come out, and the ground cover meant to be cut back, watered, encouraged to flourish.

But miracles can and do have middlemen, she decided, and then she noticed that her iced tea tasted sweeter than usual that night, though made to the same proportions, and that the cold glass did not ache her arthritis the way it usually did.

And as if to dampen this perfect balance just the moment she'd discovered it, her son, Richard, came up the walk for his bimonthly visit.

Even on a cool spring night he wore those sleeveless muscle tees—unflattering to his hairy shoulders—and sunglasses despite the fading light.

At forty-two, Richard was not a willing man, nor was he serious, unless anxious counts, and not particularly cheerful or helpful. And she had no more money to lend him, and would not if she could.

He stood on her porch step, a cigarette tucked high in the crook of his first two fingers.

"Hi, Mom."

"So? What do you think?"

"About what?"

▶ *Who was the third person Trevor helped?*

"The garden."

He spun on the heels of his two-tone leather boots, and flipped his dark glasses up to the top of his thin hairline. "You paid somebody. I told you I'd do it."

"I didn't pay."

"You did it yourself? Come on. You can't even make a fist."

"The neighbor boy did it for free."

"Very funny."

"He did."

"It must've taken hours."

"He's been working for days. You haven't been around."

"I told you I'd do it."

"Yes. You told me. But you didn't do it."

He walked inside and flipped on the t.v. to a M.A.S.H. rerun, and though she called after him to extinguish his cigarette, he failed to hear her, or pretended not to.

* * *

At first Trevor had just come by to talk, and that was good enough, and Mrs. Greenberg had never expected more. She always offered him a glass of cherry Kool-Aid, which she bought specially for him, and he'd sit at her kitchen table and talk to her. About school mostly, and football, and then a special project he had thought up for his Social Studies class, and how he needed more people he could help, and she said she had some gardening to be done, though she couldn't afford to pay much.

He said she wasn't to pay anything at all to him, and what she paid to others needn't be money, unless that was what she had plenty of. And then he drew some circles for her on a piece of paper, with her name in one, and told her about Paying Forward.

It was a foggy Saturday morning when he came by, six o'clock sharp as promised, and they stood in the mist in the front yard.

"How is the project going so far?" she said, because she could see it was important to him, a subject he liked to talk a lot about.

His brow furrowed, and he said, "Not so good, Mrs. Greenberg. Not so good." He said, "Do you think

◄ What does Richard say to his mother, Mrs. Greenberg, that he had told her before?

◄ What had Trevor first gone to Mrs. Greenberg's home to do?

that maybe people won't really Pay It Forward? That maybe they'll just say they will, or even sort of mean to, but maybe something'll go wrong, or maybe they'll just never get around to it?"

"I can only in truth speak for myself, Trevor, and say that I really will get around to it, and take it every bit as seriously as I know you do."

▶ What does Mrs. Greenberg say to Trevor in response to his worries?

He worked all weekend, after-school and after-paper-route days on the garden, and said next week he would come around and paint her fence and window boxes and porch railing with two fresh coats of white. She could still remember his smile.

* * *

It was late dusk on The Camino. Mrs. Greenberg pulled her little grocery cart over the sidewalk cracks. She always took the same route to the same store, being comforted by sameness.

Terri was working as a checker that evening, and Matt as a bagger, two of her favorite people in the world. No more than twenty, either one of them, but quick with a smile for an older woman, no <u>condescension</u>, always thinking to ask about her day, her arthritis, and still listening when she gave the answer.

▶ Who are Matt and Terri?

Terri and Matt, that's two, who probably could be counted on to pass it along, and maybe that nice lady at the North County Animal Shelter for Cats would make a fitting third. Richard would have a cow, but maybe tough love was just what he needed.

Matt said, "Nice to see you so happy tonight, Mrs. Greenberg." And he loaded her little cart carefully, so it would balance just right.

▶ What does Matt say to Mrs. Greenberg? What does he do?

It would be nice to see Matt and Terri happy, though by design she would not be around to see it. Young people needed a little nest egg, for college maybe, though it would not be enough for tuition, maybe books and clothes, or whatever they might

---

words for everyday use

con • de • scen • sion (kän də sen′ shən) *n.,* patronizing attitude or behavior, such as talking down to someone. *Mr. Briggs never treated his students with <u>condescension</u>, even when they took a long time to understand a new concept.*

choose to spend it for, because she felt they could both be trusted.

And that nice lady at the cat shelter, she would put it right back into spaying and neutering and other vet costs. No doubting her priorities.

Yes, she thought, back out in the crisp, clean-smelling night. It's right. She'd make the calls first thing in the morning.

So now maybe it seems like those three little things couldn't add up to changing the world, but you'd be surprised. At first Trevor thought it wasn't working at all, but things were happening out there, things he couldn't see. People were paying it forward whether he knew it or not. And soon Pay It Forward became a movement that surprised even Trevor.

The most important thing I can add from my own observations is this: Knowing it started from unremarkable circumstances should be a comfort to us all. Because it proves that you don't need much to change the entire world for the better. You can start with the most ordinary ingredients. You can start with the world you've got.

◄ *What does the narrator observe about Trevor's project?*

Critical Thinking

1. In your own words, explain Trevor's idea of "paying it forward." Do you think his goal of everybody getting helped more than once is feasible? Why, or why not?
2. Of the three people Trevor helped, who do you think received the greatest benefit? Give reasons for your answer.
3. Using specific examples, compare and contrast Trevor's "Pay it Forward" scheme to Stargirl's way of helping others. Do you favor one method over the other? Why or why not?

"Are Good Deeds Dead?"
by Marja Mills

ABOUT THE RELATED READING

The article "Are Good Deeds Dead?" appeared in the Chicago Tribune on October 24, 2000. The article is a review of the movie *Pay It Forward,* which was based on the novel *Pay It Forward* by Catherine Ryan Hyde. The review talks about the movie and also offers opinions about the idea behind the story. The author's opinion is that when people are requested to do good deeds, the deed itself may seem less powerful because it wasn't spontaneous. It also looks at groups that have organized around the idea of "paying it forward" or "random acts of kindness."

The Random Acts of Kindness Foundation develops materials for communities and schools and works with other organizations to set up local programs. The foundation is also part of the World Kindness Movement, an umbrella group that includes foundations in many other countries.

Are Good Deeds Dead?

In the new movie "Pay It Forward," a sad-eyed 7th grader in Las Vegas comes up with a formula for spreading kindness. He even plots it on the blackboard.

If he did a good deed for three people, helping them accomplish something they couldn't do on their own, and they each "paid it forward" by doing a good turn for three other people, the acts of kindess would multiply and gather momentum. That first good deed would be a lone pebble that pings down a mountain and sets in motion a thundering avalanche.

With its high concept and <u>melodramatic</u> ending, set to the lyrics of "Calling All Angels," the movie seems

▶ *According to the author, what does the movie seem designed to do?*

words for everyday use
melo • dra • mat • ic (me lə drə ma' tik) *adj.,* appealing to the emotions; sensational. *The <u>melodramatic</u> advertisement suggested that if a child didn't have a Craftola art kit, he or she would never blossom into the artist he or she could have been.*

designed to be a call to action, a cousin to what sometimes is called the Random Acts of Kindness movement. But there's a funny thing about the Random Acts of movement: It's not as random as it seems.

Consider next month's <u>oxymoron</u> of planned <u>spontaneity</u>: the Sixth Annual Random Acts of Kindness Week.

Sixth annual? A designated week? (Nov. 6–13). Sounds more like planned kindness than random kindness.

Perhaps it is a sign of the times that efforts to promote individual acts of kindness are organized to the point that we have the Pay It Forward Foundation, the Random Acts of Kindness Foundation, and Kindness Inc., another non-profit promoting demonstrations of kindness. All were formed within the last several years.

Like child's play, simple acts of kindness would seem to be the kind of natural, even impulsive, thing that is immune from being scheduled, organized, institutionalized.

Isn't this just something people take it upon themselves to do for their neighbors, their relatives, the occasional stranger on the train?

But then look at how, in just a few generations, modern life has transformed play from spontaneous pick-up ball on the corner to kids' soccer leagues and play dates.

"Earlier generations did this just out of normal, everyday courtesy and they didn't have to be told about committing an act of kindess," said Chuck Wall, a business professor and leading proponent of the acts-of-kindness movement.

◀ According to Chuck Wall, what didn't earlier generations have to be told?

"A neighbor needed help, you helped," Wall said. "It has (become) more difficult because we live almost anonymously in very densely populated communities. We don't even know our neighbors . . .

---

words for everyday use

oxy • mor • on (ak si mōr' än) n., combination of contradictory words. *The terms "deafening silence," "guest host," "modern history," and "old news" are <u>oxymorons</u>.*

spon • ta • ne • ity (spän tə nā' ə tē) n., quality of acting naturally, on impulse, without external constraint. *Father acted with <u>spontaneity</u> when he bid on the tractor at the auction.*

People don't reach out like they used to to help each other."

Wall garnered national attention in 1993, when he assigned his business class at Bakersfield College in California to go out and commit "senseless acts of kindness" and then write about the experience. The assignment struck a chord and made the news.

▶ What did Wall do in 1993?

Wall, who is blind, got the idea while listening to the radio. When a newscaster reported another "act of senseless violence," Wall wondered what would happen if he substituted "kindness" for "violence" in that equation.

In no time, Oprah Winfrey caught the fever and had Wall on the show to spread his message to her millions. Popular books by other authors promoted similar ideas.

It remains to be seen what new "pay-it-forward" projects are in the offing. Some schools already have taken up the idea.

On the kindness front, though, we can buy Kindness Coordinator Kits, Random Acts of Kindness lapel pins and, naturally, Random Acts of Kindness T-shirts. Not to mention the removable Random Acts of Kindness tattoos.

We have conferences on the topic, a growing stack of books about it, Web sites. Across the country and around the calendar, scores of communities have designated their own Random Acts of Kindness day.

"It does take the randomness out of it," said Wall. "But a premeditated act of kindess is not all bad either."

▶ According to the author, what is it hard to argue against?

It's hard to argue against kindness, after all, especially in a country many see as rude, rushed, awash in affluence and violence. The acts-of-kindess ventures have registered with students young and old, communities big and small, and resulted in all kinds of worthy deeds.

---

words
for
everyday
use

dis • par • age (di spar′ əj) v., speak lowly about; lower or degrade. *Lowell disparaged my speech, saying I had done a poor job, even though he didn't have to do one himself.* disparagingly, *adv.*

Even skeptics who speak disparagingly of "do-gooders" and "goodie-goodies" have to give that to the movement.

You know the kind of random acts: raking leaves for an older neighbor, paying the toll for the car behind you, reaching into your wallet when you pass a homeless person.

One appeal of those sorts of person-to-person good deeds just might be that they tend to be rarer these days, especially when it comes to doing a good turn for a neighbor.

Tom Smith has tracked Americans' attitudes toward their neighbors as part of the General Social Survey he directs at the University of Chicago's National Opinion Research Center.

"I think the shift in charity was that if you lived in a neighborhood or small town 30 or 40 years ago and you knew someone down the street and the husband was thrown out of work or disabled, you might help him out in some way," Smith said. "It was personal volunteer work more than giving money.

"I think now those things are done less on a person-to-person level, but more of it is done through organized charity efforts."

That means people have fewer obligations in their immediate surroundings, but also fewer opportunities to find satisfaction in lending a hand. "There is that very strong emotional gain that you get from seeing the good you've done," Smith said.

For his part, Wall said he is thrilled to have the idea of person-to-person good deeds lit up on movie marquees across the country.

"This movie that's just coming out is, I think, an outstanding example to demonstrate kindness is not a fringe element," Wall said. "A major movie coming out with that theme demonstrates that kindness is a major theme".

Certainly, efforts to promote good deeds and small acts of courtesy always have been around. There's the matter of organized religion, for starters.

The official slogan of the Boy Scouts of America, dating back to its founding in 1910, is "Do a good

◀ *What does Tom Smith say has changed in American attitudes?*

turn daily." (Not to be confused with the organization's official motto, "Be prepared.")

The movie's Web site, www.payitforward.com, has the usual Hollywood photos of stars Haley Joel Osment, who plays the 7th grader; Kevin Spacey, who is his lonely teacher; and Helen Hunt, the boy's mother.

But the site also links to the Pay It Forward Foundation, with oodles of ideas for committing good deeds.

In fact, the Pay It Forward Foundation came about just this summer, a few months after Catherine Ryan Hyde's novel, "Pay It Forward," hit bookstores. The movie, based on the book, opened over the weekend. With Hyde as a trustee, the foundation promotes pay-it-forward projects in schools.

▶ What acts of kindness has Catherine Ryan Hyde done?

"A small act of kindness can go a long way," Hyde says on the site. "A few things I've done are anonymously leaving breakfast every morning on the porch of an elderly local woman who had broken her wrist. Giving my truck to a younger friend when I bought a better car . . . And, of course, assisting people with car trouble."

▶ How was the idea for Hyde's novel born?

Strangers helped Hyde with her own car trouble 20 years ago one Los Angeles night. They left before she could thank them, and Hyde began looking for ways to do favors for other people. And the idea for her novel was born.

Hyde said she thinks the filmmakers snapped up the story because of its mix of optimism and grit. "It was something that had that optimistic feeling that people are saying they want and yet it was grounded in very gritty characters and almost a dark reality. So it wasn't so sweet you could die."

The movie owes a little something to "Grand Canyon," the 1991 movie starring Danny Glover and Kevin Kline. Glover plays an African-American tow truck driver who helps out Kline, a white driver with car trouble who is stranded in a rough neighborhood and being threatened.

"I really think there was a little bit of influence on my writing from 'Grand Canyon,'" Hyde said. "After

I saw it, I thought I would like to write something that big about how interconnected we are."

Now, moviegoers can go online and record their own ideas for paying it forward, then send it on to the organization.

No doubt it is only a matter of time before someone schedules National Pay It Forward Day.

Critical Thinking

1. How have society's ideas of charity shifted over the past few generations? What reasons can you give for this shift?
2. Imagine that Stargirl is reading this article. What do you think her reaction would be to an Annual Random Acts of Kindness Week?
3. Reread the article's last sentence. What point is the author trying to make? Do you agree or disagree with her?

Creative Writing Activities

Interview

Imagine you are the host of the *Hot Seat*. Prepare a list of questions that you would ask Stargirl. Include questions about her family, her values, and her likes and dislikes. Then imagine that you are Stargirl and write out responses to your questions in her voice, as you'd expect her to answer. Repeat the activity using Hillari as your *Hot Seat* guest.

Story Continuation

What happened to Stargirl after she left Arizona? With your classmates, brainstorm a list of new challenges or difficulties Stargirl might encounter. Choose one and write one chapter that details this new experience. You may or may not wish to include other characters from *Stargirl*.

Critique

Characterization is the act of creating or describing a character. Writers create character using three major techniques: by showing what characters say, do, or think; by showing what other characters say or think about them; and by describing what physical features, dress, and personality the characters display. Brainstorm ideas with which Spinelli created the character of Stargirl. Write an essay in which you critique Spinelli's effectiveness in creating a believable character. Use examples from the novel to support your claims.

Letter

Imagine you are Leo, fifteen years after breaking up with Stargirl. Write her a letter in which you explain why you did not ask her to the Ocotillo Ball. Tell Stargirl what you've been doing since that time and how you feel about Stargirl now.

Critical Writing Activities

The Changing Character of Stargirl

How does Stargirl change throughout the course of the novel? Is she the same Stargirl she was when she first began high school in Arizona? Why, or why not? Write an essay in which you address these questions.

Individuality, Fitting In, Blessings

In this novel, themes about individuality, fitting in, and blessings come up frequently. In a brief essay, address one of these issues. You may wish to address how Stargirl's view of individuality differs from Leo's, how Stargirl discovers that fitting in is not always the most comfortable role, or whether or not you would define Stargirl's presence at Mica High School as a blessing.

Compare and Contrast

Leo learns new ways of looking at himself and life from both Stargirl and Archie. Are the two teachers similar? Are they effective in their teachings to Leo? Write an essay in which you compare and contrast the two.

Suspense

Stargirl is full of suspense. Examine how Spinelli uses suspense throughout this novel. You may wish to pay special attention to chapter endings and refer back to your responses to the Understanding Literature question on suspense after chapter 22 on page 106.

Projects

Mock *Hot Seat*

Hold your own *Hot Seat* show. One student can play the host, another can play Stargirl, and others can play the jurors. Instead of having the trial take place at the time it did during the story, however, pretend the show is airing earlier—during the height of Stargirl's popularity. Ask questions that will help students better understand who Stargirl is.

Enchanted Place

Find your own enchanted place. Find a spot where you can try meditating, or clearing your mind of everything and focusing on nothing. Experiment with various places until you find a place where you feel most relaxed and comfortable. Turn off your senses and let the earth speak to you. Before you begin, you may wish to go back and read Stargirl's description of doing nothing on pages 77–80.

Books About Individuality

Did you enjoy this book? Would you like to read other books that cover the theme of individuality? Find at least ten other young-adult novels or short stories that are about individuality. You might start by asking friends or relatives to remember books they've read that cover this theme. Once you've gathered ten titles, compile a bibliography of your findings. Choose one of the titles to read. Write a brief essay that compares it to *Stargirl*.

Extinct Birds

Research and compare two extinct birds, such as the passenger pigeon and the moa. For each bird you choose, find out where it lived, what it ate, and learn about its life cycle. Compare and contrast your findings in a written report. Share your findings with the class.

Glossary of Words for Everyday Use

PRONUNCIATION KEY

VOWEL SOUNDS

a	hat	ō	go	ə	extra
ā	play	ȯ, ô	paw, born		under
ä	star	u̇	book, put		civil
e	then	ü, o͞o	blue, stew		honor
ē	me	oi	boy		bogus
i	sit	ou	wow		
ī	my	u	up		

CONSONANT SOUNDS

b	but	l	lip	t	sit
ch	watch	m	money	th	with
d	do	n	on	v	valley
f	fudge	ŋ	song, sink	w	work
g	go	p	pop	y	yell
h	hot	r	rod	z	pleasure
j	jump	s	see		
k	brick	sh	she		

abrupt (ə brəpt') *adj.*, without preparation or warning; unexpected.

ab • surd (əb sərd') *n.*, something that is clearly ridiculous.

ac • clam • a • tion (a klə mā' shən) *n.*, overwhelming affirmative vote by cheers, shouts, or applause.

ac • quire (ə kwir') *v.*, get.

am • ble (am' bəl) *v.*, go at an easy pace; saunter.

amok (ə mək') *adv.*, undisciplined, uncontrolled, or faulty manner.

amor • phous (ə mȯr' fəs) *adj.*, having no definite form.

an • ni • hi • late (a nī' ə lāt') *v.*, destroy completely.

an • tic (an' tik) *n.*, attention-drawing act or action.

baf • fle • ment (ba' fəl ment) *n.*, confusing or puzzling.

balk (bȯk') *v.*, refuse abruptly.

ban • ish (ba' nish) *v.*, drive out or remove from a place.

bar • ren (bār' ən) *adj.*, producing inferior or scarce vegetation.

bi • zarre (bə zär') *adj.*, strikingly out of the ordinary.

blithe (blīth') *adj.*, cheerful, carefree.

bog • gle (bä' gəl) *v.*, start with fright or amazement.

boon • docks (bün' däks) *n.*, rough country filled with dense brush.

cas • cade (kas kād') *v.*, fall.

cha • rade (shə rād') *n.*, empty or deceptive act.

chis • eled (chi' zəld) *adj.*, formed or crafted as if with a chisel.

con • de • scen • sion (kän də sen' shən) *n.*, patronizing attitude or behavior, such as talking down to someone.

con • fer (kən fer') *v.*, meet for discussion; have a conference.

con • found (kən found') *v.*, mix up indiscriminately; to baffle, stupefy, perplex, or confuse.

con • trary (c trer ē) *adj.*, opposite.

con • vene (kən vēn') vi., come together in a body.

con • verge (kən vʉrj') *vi.*, come together.

con • voy (kän' vȯi) *n.*, protective escort.

de • fi • ance (də fī' əns) *n.*, open disregard for authority or opposition.

de • lu • sion (di loo' zhən) *n.*, incorrect perception of reality.

der • e • lict (der' ə likt) *adj.*, abandoned.

de • tect • able (di tek' tə bəl) *adj.*, able to be determined or noticed.

di • lap • i • dat • ed (də la' pə dāt əd) *adj.*, decayed or deteriorated through neglect or misuse.

dis • dain • ful (dis dān' fəl) *adj.*, to be full of scorn or contempt.

dis • em • bark (dis' im bärk') *v.*, leave a means of transportation.

dis • lodge (dis läj') *v.*, force out of a secure or settled position.

dis • par • age (di spar' əj) *v.*, speak lowly about; lower or degrade.

dis • tin • guish (di stin' gwish) *v.*, to discern; to detect with the eyes or with other senses.

dor • mant (dôr' mənt) *adj.*, inoperative; inactive.

elat • ed (ē lāt' ed) *adj.*, filled with joy.

elu • sive (ē lōō′ siv) *adj.*, not easily seen or understood.

em • pa • thy (em′ pǝ thē) *n.*, ability to share in another's emotions.

en • vy (en′ vē) *v.*, feel resentful awareness of an advantage enjoyed by another joined with a desire to possess the same advantage.

es • teem (is tēm′) *n.*, high regard.

ex • ot • ic (ek so′ tik) *adj.*, not native to the place where found; foreign; exciting or mysterious.

ex • pec • ta • tion (ek spek tā shǝn) *n.*, anticipation.

fac • e • tious (fǝ sē′ shǝs) *adj.*, witty in a playful but often inappropriate manner.

fa • na • tic (fǝ nat′ ik) *n.*, person who holds extreme and unreasonable views; zealot.

fes • toon (fes tōōn′) *vt.*, adorn or hang with a wreath or garland of flowers.

flour • ish (flǝr′ ish) *v.*, wave in the air.

gan • der (gan′ dǝr) *n.*, look, glance.

gape (gāp) *v.*, gaze stupidly or in openmouthed surprise or wonder.

grav • i • tate (gra′ vǝ tāt′) *vi.*, move toward something.

grim (grim′) *adj.*, somber, gloomy.

gump • tion (gǝm(p)′ shǝn) *n.*, shrewd common sense, courage, and initiative.

hap • less (ha′ plǝs) *adj.*, unfortunate.

heft (heft′) *n.*, weight, heaviness.

hot • bed (hät′ bed) *n.*, environment that favors rapid growth or development.

hov • er (hǝ′ ver) *v.*, stay suspended in the air near one place.

im • mob • i • lize (i mō′ bǝ līz′) *v.*, reduce or eliminate motion of the body or a body part.

im • promp • tu (im präm′ tü) *adj.*, without preparation or advance thought.

imp • ish (im' pish) *adj.*, mischievous.

im • pul • sive (im pəl' siv) *adj.*, spontaneous.

in • ci • den • tal • ly (in sə den' təl ē) *adv.*, by way of interjection, by the way.

in • qui • si • tion (in' qwə zish' ən) *n.*, severe or intensive questioning.

in • tense (in ten(t)s') *adj.*, very strong, extreme.

in • tent (in tent') *adj.*, earnest, fixed.

in • ter • ro • gate (in ter' ə gāt') *v.*, ask questions of.

in • tro • vert (in' trə vərt') *n.*, reserved or shy person.

is • o • la • tion (ī' sə lā' shən) *n.*, condition of being apart from others.

ju • bi • la • tion (jōō' bə lā' shən) *n.*, rejoicing.

keen (kēn') *adj.*, sharp, intense.

lib • er • a • tion (li bə rā' shən) *n.*, act of setting free.

lure (loor') *n.*, temptation.

ma • roon (mə' rün) *v.*, place or leave in isolation or without hope of ready escape.

mas • o • chis • tic (ma' sə kis' tik) *adj.*, quality of taking pleasure in suffering.

mas • sa • cre (ma' si kər) *n.*, act of complete destruction.

med • dle (med' əl) *v.*, interfere in something that is not one's business.

melo • dra • mat • ic (me lə drə ma' tik) *adj.*, appealing to the emotions; sensational.

met • ro • nom • ic (me trə nä' mik) *adj.*, mechanically regular.

mis • chie • vous (mis' chə vəs) *adj.*, irresponsibly playful.

mon • u • men • tal (män' yə men' təl) *adj.*, outstanding; very great.

mor • bid (môr' bəd) *adj.*, abnormally susceptible to or characterized by gloomy or unwholesome feelings.

mor • ti • fied (môrt' ə fīd) *adj.*, shamed, humiliated.

mull (məl′) *v.,* consider at length; ponder.

noble (nō′ bəl) *adj.,* possessing excellent qualities.

non • con • for • mi • ty (nän′ kən fôr′ mə tē) *n.,* refusal to conform to an established creed, rule, or practice.

obliv • i • ous (ə bli′ vē əs) *adj.,* unaware; lacking attention.

ob • scure (äb skyur′) *adj.,* unclear or unknown.

op • ti • mism (äp′ tə məsm) *n.,* inclination to believe in the best possible outcomes for any situation or event.

or • a • tor • i • cal (ôr ə tôr′ i kəl) *adj.,* relating to one distinguished for skill and power as a public speaker.

oxy • mor • on (ak si mōr′ än) *n.,* combination of contradictory words.

pan • to • mime (pan′ tə mīm) *n.,* dramatic presentation given without words, using only action and gestures.

per • pet • u • al (pər pə′ chə wəl′) *adj.,* continuing forever.

pre • am • ble (prē′ am bəl) *n.,* introductory statement.

prim (prim′) *adj.,* stiffly formal and proper.

pri • mor • di • al (pri mər′ dē əl) *adj.,* existing at the beginning; first in time.

pro • claim (prō klām′) *v.,* announce.

prom • e • nade (prä mə nād′) *n.,* place for strolling.

prom • i • nent (prä′ mə nənt) *adj.,* standing out, conspicuous.

rab • id (ra′ bəd) *adj.,* going to extreme lengths in expressing a feeling, interest, or opinion.

rap • ture (rap′ chər) *n.,* great pleasure.

rau • cous (rô′ kəs) *adj.,* loud and disorderly.

re • cruit (ri krüt′) *v.,* enlist new members.

re • luc • tance (ri lək′ tən(t)s) *n.,* unwillingness.

re • luc • tant (ri lək′ tənt) *adj.,* not in the mood, disinclined.

re • pent (ri pent′) *v.,* feel regret or change one's mind; turn from sin.

re • sume (ri zōōm′) *v.,* take, get, or occupy again.

ren • der (ren' dər) *v.*, present or submit.

rev • el (re' vəl) *v.*, take immense pleasure.

riv • et • ing (ri' və tiŋ) *adj.*, engrossing, fascinating.

scarce • ly (skers' lē) *adv.*, almost not.

seethe (sēth') *v.*, be in a state of rapid agitated movement; suffer violent internal excitement.

ser • e • nade (ser' ə nād') *v.*, perform a complimentary vocal or instrumental piece of music.

shun (shən') *v.*, avoid deliberately.

spec • u • late (spek' yü lāt) *v.*, take to be true without solid evidence.

splay (splā') *v.*, spread outward.

spon • ta • ne • ity (spän tə nā' ə tē) *n.*, quality of acting naturally, on impulse, without external constraint.

spright • ly (sprīt' lē) *adj.*, full of energy and spirit.

sti • fle (stī' fəl) *v.*, hold back, stop, smother.

stoke (stōk') *v.*, stir up or feed fuel to.

strat • um (strā' təm) *n.*, sheetlike mass of sedimentary rock or earth of one kind lying between beds of other kinds.

sub • dued (sub dood') *adj.*, controlled or repressed emotionally.

sul • len (sə' lən) *adj.*, gloomy, somber.

sup • press (sə pres') *v.*, inhibit; put down by force.

ten • ta • tive (tən' tə tiv) *adj.*, hesitant; uncertain.

tor • rent (tôr' ənt) *n.*, swift, violent stream.

tra • verse (tra vərs') *v.*, travel across or move through.

trea • son (trē' zən) *n.*, betrayal of a trust.

un • der • mine (ən dər mīn') *v.*, weaken or ruin.

un • rav • el (ən ra' vəl) *v.*, come apart.

un • re • spons • ive (un rē spän' siv) *adj.*, not quick to respond or react with sympathy; insensitive.

un • shack • le (ən sha' kəl) *v.*, free from shackles.

va • cant (vā kənt) *adj.*, not occupied; empty.

vague (vāg') *adj.,* not clearly expressed.

va • moose (və müs') *v.,* depart quickly.

var • i • ant (ver' ē ənt) *n.,* something that differs from the standard form.

veer (vir') *v.,* change direction.

vi • tal • i • ty (vī tal' ə tē) *n.,* energy; life.

vic • tim • ize (vik' tə mīz') *v.,* subject to deception or fraud.

wa • ver (wā' vər) *v.,* sway unsteadily.

writhe (rīth') *v.,* twist or turn.

wry (rī) *adj.,* ironic or sarcastic; grimly humorous.

zeal (zēal) *n.,* eagerness, enthusiasm.

Handbook of Literary Terms

CONFLICT. A **conflict** is a struggle between two people or things in a literary work.

DESCRIPTION. A **description** portrays a character, an object, or a scene. Descriptions make use of sensory details—words and phrases that describe how things look, sound, smell, taste, or feel.

DIALOGUE. **Dialogue** is conversation involving two or more people or characters.

FLASHBACK. A **flashback** is a part of a story, poem, or play that presents events that happened at an earlier time.

FORESHADOWING. **Foreshadowing** is the act of hinting at events that will happen later in a poem, story, or play.

IRONY OF SITUATION. **Irony of situation** is an event that contradicts the expectations of the characters, the reader, or the audience of a literary work.

METAPHOR. A **metaphor** is a figure of speech in which one thing is spoken or written about as if it were another. This figure of speech invites the reader to make a comparison between the two things.

MOOD. **Mood,** or **atmosphere** is the emotion created in the reader by a piece of writing. A writer creates a mood through the use of concrete details.

NARRATOR. A **narrator** is a person or character who tells a story. Works of fiction almost always use a narrator. The narrator in a work of fiction may be a major or minor character or simply someone who witnessed or heard about the events being related.

RESOLUTION. The **resolution** is the point at which the central conflict is ended, or resolved.

SIMILE. A **simile** is a comparison using *like* or *as*.

SUSPENSE. **Suspense** is a feeling of expectation, anxiousness, or curiosity created by questions raised in the mind of the reader or viewer.

THEME. A **theme** is a central idea in a literary work.

Acknowledgments

"The Origin of Plumage" from *Myths of the Iroquois.* Reprinted by permission of Iroqrafts LTD, Tuscarora Road. Reader's Resource #2, Ohsweken, Ontario, Canada N0Zz1M0.

"Passports to Understanding" from *Wouldn't Take Nothing for My Journey Now* by Maya Angelou, © 1993 by Maya Angelou. Used by permission of Random House, Inc.

"New Love" from *Fresh Paint* by Eve Merriam. Copyright © 1986 Eve Merriam. Used by permission of Marian Reiner.

From *Pay It Forward* by Catherine Ryan Hyde. Copyright © 1999 by Catherine Ryan Hyde. Excerpted, with slight changes, by permission of Simon & Schuster Adult Publishing Group. Used with permission.

Chicago Tribune. "Are Good Deeds Dead?" by Marja Mills, from the Chicago Tribune, dated October 24, 2000. Copyright © 2000, Chicago Tribune Company. All rights reserved. Used with permission.